INSIGHT GUIDES

EXPLORE

BANGKOK

PLAN & BOOK
YOUR TAILOR-MADE TRIP

BRAZIL CHILE ECUADOR

TAILOR-MADE TRIPS & UNIQUE EXPERIENCES CREATED BY LOCAL TRAVEL EXPERTS AT INSIGHTGUIDES.COM/HOLIDAYS

Insight Guides has been inspiring travellers with high-quality travel content for over 45 years. As well as our popular guidebooks, we now offer the opportunity to book tailor-made private trips completely personalised to your needs and interests. By connecting with one of our local experts, you will directly benefit from their expertise and local know-how, helping you create memories that will last a lifetime.

HOW INSIGHTGUIDES.COM/HOLIDAYS WORKS

STEP 1

Pick your dream destination and submit an enquiry, or modify an existing itinerary if you prefer.

STEP 2

Fill in a short form, sharing details of your travel plans and preferences with a local expert.

STEP 3

Your local expert will create your personalised itinerary, which you can amend until you are completely satisfied.

STEP 4

Book securely online. Pack your bags and enjoy your holiday! Your local expert will be available to answer questions during your trip.

BENEFITS OF PLANNING & BOOKING AT INSIGHTGUIDES.COM/HOLIDAYS

PLANNED BY LOCAL EXPERTS
The Insight Guides local experts are hand-picked, based on their experience in the travel industry and their impeccable standards of customer service.

SAVE TIME & MONEY
When a local expert plans your trip, you save time and money when you book, even during high season. You won't be charged for using a credit card either.

TAILOR-MADE TRIPS
Book with Insight Guides, and you will be in complete control of the planning process, from the initial selections to amending your final itinerary.

BOOK & TRAVEL STRESS-FREE
Enjoy stress-free travel when you use the Insight Guides secure online booking platform. All bookings come with a money-back guarantee.

WHAT OTHER TRAVELLERS THINK ABOUT TRIPS BOOKED AT INSIGHTGUIDES.COM/HOLIDAYS

Trip to Portugal

Every step of the planning process and the trip itself was effortless and exceptional. Our special interests, preferences and requests were accommodated resulting in a trip that exceeded our expectations.

Corinne, USA   ★★★★★

Trip to Vietnam

The organization was superb, the drivers professional, and accommodation quite comfortable. I was well taken care of! My thanks to your colleagues who helped make my trip to Vietnam such a great experience.

Heather   ★★★★★

DON'T MISS OUT
BOOK NOW AT
INSIGHTGUIDES.COM/HOLIDAYS

CONTENTS

ARCHITECTURE

Explore Dusit's Thai-Euro grandeur (route 5), the splendour of royal Rattanakosin (route 1), towering spires and stupas at Wat Arun and Wat Pho (route 2) or faded colonial designs at Tha Oriental (route 2).

RECOMMENDED ROUTES FOR...

CHILDREN

Kids will love the tropical fish at Sea Life Bangkok (route 7) and taking an express boat ride up the Chao Phraya River (route 11).

ESCAPING THE CROWDS

Tap in to Ko Kret's rural pace of life (route 11), see the waterfall at Erawan National Park (route 13) or explore the quiet canals of Thonburi (route 3).

CULINARY DELIGHTS

Catch the heady aromas of Chinatown's steaming food stalls (route 6), savour seafood by the seaside at Hua Hin and Pattaya (route 17 and route 18), or hunt out sky high flavours in Silom (route 8).

HANDS-ON CULTURE

Watch Thai boxing at Channel 7 Boxing Stadium (route 10), or learn the techniques from the masters at Sor Vorapin gym (route 9), then heal your aches with a Thai massage course at Wat Pho (route 2).

HISTORY FANS

Marvel at the Chakri legacy of Rattanakosin (route 1), the ancient capital Ayutthaya (route 15), Old City temples (route 4) and the eternal bustle of Chinatown (route 6).

NIGHT OWLS

Drink beers at backpacker bars in Banglamphu (route 9), go go-go mad in Patpong (route 8) or Pattaya (route 18), or shop until late in Patpong Night Market (route 8).

OUTDOOR ENTHUSIASTS

Trek in the jungle near Kanchanaburi (route 13) or cycle around compact Ko Kret (route 11).

INTRODUCTION

An introduction to Bangkok's geography, customs and culture, plus illuminating background information on cuisine, history and what to do when you're there.

Bangkok's skyline

EXPLORE BANGKOK

Cosmopolitan Bangkok blends evocative street markets with glitzy modern malls, Buddhist philosophy with animism, and traditional reserve with lashings of sanuk (fun). The result is an effervescent milieu that draws visitors by the million.

With an area of 1,565 sq km (604 sq miles), Bangkok is over 30 times larger than any other city in Thailand and has a population of about 6 million (10–12 million in the greater metropolitan area). Although it is increasingly globalised and has readily adopted Western, Chinese and Japanese influences, the city remains steeped in its own fabulously rich culture and beliefs.

CITY OF ANGELS

Until the mid-18th century Bangkok was a duty port for tall ships bearing the world's cargoes, bound for the capital, Ayutthaya, 76km (48 miles) up-river. At the time it was a small but growing community called Bang Makok (Village of Wild Plums), although even by the 16th century it was already designated a town rather than a mere village. After the destruction of Ayutthaya, following a siege by the Burmese in 1767, the new king, Taksin, chose Thonburi, on the opposite river bank to Bang Makok, as his new capital.

Taksin was overthrown in 1782, and his successor King Rama I moved the capital across the river, digging canals to form the artificial island, Ko Rattanakosin, which

he planned in the image of Ayutthaya. After building the stunning Grand Palace, he chose an equally stunning name for his new city – Krungthepmahanakhon Amonrattanakosin Mahintharayutthaya Mahadilokphop Nopphosin Ratchathani-burirom Udomrathaniwetmahasa Amon-phiman Awatansathit Sakkathatiya Witsanukamprasit, or 'City of Angels, Great City of Immortals, Magnificent City of the Nine Gems, Seat of the King, City of Royal Palaces, Home of the Gods Incarnate, Erected by Visvakarman at Indra's Behest'. It is the longest place name in the world. Thais call it Krung Thep (City of Angels), for short, while foreigners stick close to the original settlement's centuries-old name.

CITY LAYOUT

The low-lying capital grew slowly; it was a city of canals and elephant paths, with communities dwelling outside the old walls of Rattanakosin in Phra Nakorn (the Old City) and along the river in Chinatown and Dusit. Rapid 20th-century expansion – particularly from the economic boom in the 1980s – has resulted in a population 10 times bigger than that

Bangkok floating market

during World War II; today, one in every six Thais lives here. Modern Bangkok has no definitive city centre, with major business and shopping areas now occupying Pathumwan, Silom and Sukhumvit. Across the river, in parts of Thonburi, canals thread past temples and wooden houses for a glimpse of earlier times.

Navigating the city

Bangkok has major daytime traffic problems, one reason being that many roads are built over old canals, so they are often narrow. A network of expressways alleviates some of the city's major daytime problems, it is better when possible to travel by either the overhead Skytrain or the underground MRT systems, both of which are being extended.

That said, air-conditioned taxis are comfortable, metered and inexpensive by international standards. Tuk tuks are fun, but rarely cheaper than taxis, and motorcycle taxis are quick, but nerve wracking, and you are exposed to traffic fumes. Buses cost just a few baht but have little English signage (tourism booths have bus maps). A pleasant and airy alternative is to travel by river, either by express boat to major piers or by longtail boat along the canals.

Exploring on foot

Walking is an adventure. The colourful streets give a peek into everyday life as you pick your way through vendors selling all manner of goods from stalls, wheeled carts and blankets on the ground. The going is easier in the older parts of the city, but you will still be walking in the heat. Make use of the many convenience stores and itinerant traders to buy water or fruit; the latter is ready-cut in a bag with a cocktail stick so it is easy to eat on the move. And take your time: there is a good reason why the local people walk so slowly.

Four routes in this book – Rattanakosin, The Old City, Wat Arun and Wat Pho, and Banglamphu – are in and around the original walled city. The edges of some routes are close to the edges of others, so it is easy to mix and match the attractions.

FAITH AND BELIEFS

The postcard images of Buddhist monks in saffron robes may be clichéd, but

What's a wat?

You will see *wats*, or Buddhist temples, everywhere in Bangkok. Other common architectural terms include: *bot* – the ordination hall of a temple, where religious rites are held; *viharn* – a replica of the *bot* that is used to keep Buddha images; *prang* – an ellipse-shaped stupa based on the corner tower of a Khmer temple and also housing images of the Buddha; and *chedi* (stupa) – the most venerated structure, a bell-like dome that originally enshrined relics of the Buddha, later of holy men and kings.

Wat Pho temple

they accurately reflect the importance of religion in the country. Around 95 percent of the nation subscribes to Theravada Buddhism, and there are signs of its significance everywhere, from the white bar on the national flag to Buddha images in the workplace and monks collecting alms in the street. Most men will spend at least a few days in a monastery, often following a family death, and even the monarch is required to have been ordained at some time in his life.

But Thailand, historically located on trade routes between larger powers, has always been populated by crossroads communities. As such, the people have become adept at bending under foreign influence and adapting cultural traits to suit their own needs. While Buddhism – which arrived via India and Sri Lanka – became dominant, there are still strong echoes today of Brahman beliefs that emerged from the Khmer kingdom in the East, and even today Brahman priests officiate at major ceremonies. The Thai wedding ceremony is almost entirely Brahman, as are many funeral rites. Royal ceremonies, such as the Ploughing Ceremony in May, are presided over by Brahman priests. Many pilgrimage sites are dedicated to Hindu gods, including the Erawan Shrine, and temples happily mix Buddhist and Hindu deities.

Also significant are older beliefs in animism and supernaturalism. Fortune tellers are widely visited (even by politicians), important events are organised to fall on auspicious days, and people wear tattoos that they believe will ward off danger. Objects such as buildings and trees are thought to contain spirits that must be placated lest they become agitated and return to show their displeasure. Thus, many have a spirit house or shrine where people leave offerings of food and drink to keep their occupants comfortable. It is a complex mix of beliefs that informs a large part of Thailand's unique character.

THE MONARCHY

Since 1932 Thailand has been a constitutional monarchy, in which the king exercises little formal power. However,

---

Warrior queen

One of the most famous heroines of Thai history is Queen Suriyothai, the wife of King Maha Chakapat (1548–69). Legend states that when her husband went to engage the invading Burmese armies in the first year of his reign, Queen Suriyothai disguised herself as a man and rode into battle with him. His elephant wounded, the king found himself in mortal danger, but the queen rode her elephant between him and his attacker and was herself killed. The white-and-gold Chedi Si Suriyothai stands in her honour, overlooking the river on the western edge of the city. In 2001 the film *Suriyothai* was a huge box office hit. Francis Ford Coppola edited the US release.

Inside a Chinatown temple   *Market shopping*

the monarchy is a highly visible institution, and many people displayed a genuine love for the late King Bhumibol Adulyadej (Rama IX), who ascended the throne in 1948 and was the world's longest-reigning monarch when he passed away in 2016. As well as being admired for charitable works, particularly his rural development projects, he was viewed as a moral beacon in a country where corruption is widespread. His subjects also look to him as a calming influence during recurring times of political tension and coups d'état.

He was succeeded to the throne by his son, now King Maha Vajiralongkorn (Rama X). The king's image is seen widely in homes, workplaces and official buildings, and when the national anthem is played in schools and public places, such as cinemas, people stand respectfully. Recently, Thais have taken to wearing yellow to honour the king, and, in 2007, when King Bhumibol was photographed wearing a pink shirt, within hours pink shirts were selling in their thousands across the country.

In recent years, though, the monarchy has been criticised by some supporters of the fugitive ex-prime minister Thaksin Shinawatra, who believe elements of the 'traditional elite' were involved in his overthrow. The 'lèse majesté' laws, which can lead to imprisonment for crit-

DON'T LEAVE BANGKOK WITHOUT...	
Canal touring in a longtail boat. Take to the water in Thonburi for a look at how Bangkok used to be, sliding past wooden house communities, historic temples and floating markets. See page 38.	**Shopping in Chatuchak market.** Join the 100,000 shoppers at 'the world's largest flea market'. Search hard and you'll find what you are looking for; follow your nose and you'll discover unimagined treasures. See page 70.
Relaxing with a Thai massage at Wat Pho. This ancient healing practice is believed to be based on methods developed by the Buddha's own personal physician. The learning centre is Wat Pho, Bangkok's oldest temple, and home of the stunning Reclining Buddha. See page 35.	**Visiting Wat Phra Kaew.** The fairytale royal temple attached to Bangkok's Grand Palace glitters golden in the sun. It contains several important religious buildings and the most sacred Buddha image in Thailand. See page 29.
Eating a spicy *som tam*. One of the world's great salads, this spicy-sour delight is based on green papaya. Originally an Isaan dish, it has many variations and is widely available in Bangkok. See page 17.	**Touring the Ancient City.** Leave Bangkok for the bucolic surrounds of this Thailand-shaped park with near life-size, and painstakingly accurate, replicas of important temples and palaces, including some lost centuries ago. See page 84.

Lumphini Park

icising the king, have been used more widely than usual to silence political rivals of all sides.

POWER PLAYS

Since the advent of constitutional monarchy (see above), Bangkok has witnessed many power plays. Early incidents, in 1949 and 1951, saw the army and police fighting navy-led coup attempts. Three tragic incidents centred on Thammasat University and Democracy Monument, in 1973, 1976 and 1992, caused many deaths as the police, military and private 'militias' opened fire. But since 2008 a struggle has divided the whole country. The People's Alliance for Democracy (with close ties to the military and traditional elite, wearing yellow) and the United Front for Democracy Against Dictatorship (supporters of deposed ex-prime minister Thaksin Shinawatra, wearing red) occupied places like Bangkok International Airport and the commercial district on various occasions in attempts to topple successive governments. Many deaths resulted. In 2014, the Thai army staged a coup d'état and its former general, Prayut Chan-o-cha, remains in power at the time of writing. In 2019, in the country's first election since the coup, he was voted in as prime minister by parliament after the indecisive result saw him win the popular vote but his party won fewer seats than its closest rival.

BANGKOK'S PEOPLE

Bangkok, perhaps more than most capital cities, is unrepresentative of the rest of the country. Because it has developed so rapidly, there is often a stark contrast between traditional and contemporary lifestyles, and commentators often claim that 'Thainess' and its inherent family values are breaking down in the face of globalisation. The increasingly educated and confident middle classes are blurring the lines of a conventionally hierarchical society, while the MTV generation has taken the fuel of Western and Japanese pop culture to build an ever more edgy creative energy. However, examples of traditional lifestyles thread tantalisingly through the modern landscape, often around markets and temples.

Cultural variations are brought to the capital by migrant workers from Isaan in the northeast; by the large Chinese community; and by Indians, many of whom grew rich after World War II, when they returned to find their stocks of cotton intact in the warehouses while the price had skyrocketed.

IN THE NAME OF FUN

Three concepts in the local psyche are significant in forming the Thais' relaxed attitude to life. *Jai yen* (cool heart) and *mai pen rai* (never mind) underpin the tolerance towards the capital's many fringe lifestyles. The third, *sanuk* (fun), requires that everything – work, play,

Democracy Monument

Wai greeting

tragedy – should have elements of fun, and always with lots of friends. It is this that makes Bangkok one of the world's most exhilarating cities.

TOP TIPS FOR EXPLORING BANGKOK

When to visit. The best time to visit Bangkok is during the cool season from late November to February, when temperatures range from 18–32°C (65–90°F), and it is less humid. The warm season is from March to mid-June, while the rains pour from June to October.

Land of smiles. It is often handy to keep this advertising slogan to mind. Thais lose respect for people who lose their temper. When confronted by frustrations you will get far better results by smiling through it than by raising your voice.

Shopping tactics. Outside shopping malls it is acceptable to ask if there's a discount, as some shops are happy to drop five or ten percent. In markets, watching others shop, particularly Thais, who will mostly get a better price, gives an idea of how low you can bargain.

Bargaining. Don't start bargaining unless you really want to buy. A good place to start your opening offer is around one-third of the asking price. In the end, if you pay less than what it is worth to you, it's a bargain.

Antiques. Many stalls will claim to sell antiques, but unless you know what you are doing it is best to treat such claims with a pinch of salt. Evaluate your buys according to what they mean to you, not as possible investments.

Safety. Bangkok is generally very safe for tourists, but exercising some caution is wise, particularly around red-light areas. Don't carry too much money in these bars and don't be flash with it.

Taxi scams. Don't take taxis that are parked outside hotels and tourist spots, they will always refuse to use the meter and hassle you to join them on some hopeless shopping trip, in which they make a commission. Hail one that is passing on the street.

Cheap eats. Competition is fierce in Bangkok's fast expanding service industries. Check newspapers and magazines for the latest happy hours and meal deals, which can get very cheap, especially on mid-week buffets.

Cold restaurants. Living in a steamy hot country, Thais love air conditioning. Consider taking a shawl or jacket if dining in a restaurant as the temperature is often polar and the wind gale force.

Event information. For pre-planning events before you leave, Thai Ticketmajor (tel: 0 2262 3456; www.thaiticketmajor.com) has the earliest information on what bands or shows will be visiting Thailand in the coming weeks.

Underage clubbing. You have to be over 20 to enter clubs in Thailand, and most venues require proof. To avoid disappointment always carry a copy of your passport (not the original) to prove your age, however old you look.

Thai chillies

FOOD AND DRINK

Thai cuisine is not all about tongue-searing dishes. Although the spiciness may initially be overwhelming, what is most impressive is the complex balance of flavours that lies underneath.

Whether tucked in Old City alleys or against modern blocks, street food is everywhere in Bangkok – a legion of mango sellers, roast-duck specialists and vendors hacking cleavers into crispy pork. The long-time practice of 'proper' Thai restaurants catering to tourist tastes is now challenged by a movement towards authentic traditional flavours epitomised by places such as Bo.lan (see page 111), Supanniga Eating Room (www.supannigaeatingroom.com) and a branch of Nahm (see page 115), of London, which was the world's first Michelin-starred Thai restaurant.

Despite perceptions, Thai food is not just out-and-out spicy; most meals will include a number of less aggressive dishes, some subtly flavoured only with herbs.

REGIONAL CUISINES

The variations of food and cooking styles are immense, as each of the country's four regions has a distinct cuisine of its own. The northeast is influenced by Laos, the south by Malaysia and Indonesia, the central area by the royal kitchens, and the north by Burma and Yunnan. They're all available in Bangkok, often at street stalls and markets serving migrant communities. To find a good cook, just head for the busiest stall.

Northern cuisine

This is the mildest of Thai cuisines. Northerners generally eat *khao nio* (sticky rice), kneading it into a ball to dip into sauces and curries such as the Burmese *kaeng hanglay*, a sweet and tamarind-sour pork dish.

Other specialities include sausages, such as the spicy pork *sai oua* (roasted over a coconut-husk fire to impart aroma and flavour) and *naem* (fermented raw pork and pork skin seasoned with garlic and chilli). *Laab* is a salad dish of minced pork, chicken, beef or fish served with mint leaves and raw vegetables.

Dipping sauces include *nam prik ong* (minced pork, mild chillies, tomatoes, garlic and shrimp paste) and the potent *nam prik noom* (grilled chillies, onions and garlic). Both are eaten with the popular snack called *khaep moo* (crispy pork rind).

Northeastern cuisine

Isaan food from the northeast is simple, generally spicy and eaten with sticky rice

Royal Thai cuisine   *Skewered meatballs on a street-side food stall*

kept in bamboo baskets. Dishes include *som tam* (shredded green papaya, garlic, chillies, lime juice, and variations of tomatoes, dried shrimp, preserved crab and fermented fish) and a version of *laab* that is spicier and sourer than the northern version.

The most popular Isaan dish is perhaps *gai yang*, chicken grilled in a marinade of peppercorns, garlic, fish sauce, coriander and palm sugar, and served with both hot and sweet dipping sauces.

Southern cuisine

The south has Thailand's hottest dishes. Fishermen, who needed food that would last for days at sea, are said to have created *kaeng tai plaa* by blending fermented fish stomachs with chillies, vegetables and an intensely hot sauce. Even hotter is *kaeng leuang* (yellow curry) with fish, green papaya and bamboo shoots or palm hearts. But the south also has gentler specialities such as *khao yam*, an innocuous salad of rice, vegetables, pounded dried fish and fish sauce. Slightly spicier are *phad sataw*, a stir-fry usually made with pork or shrimp, and *sataw*, a large lima bean lookalike with a strong flavour and aroma. Muslim flavours are also common, with Indian and Persian influences in items like biriyani, roti and massaman curry.

Central cuisine

Central cuisine, which has been influenced by the royal kitchens, includes many of the dishes made international-

ally famous at Thai restaurants abroad. It is notable for the use of coconut milk, which mellows the chilli heat. Trademark dishes include *tom kha gai*, a soup of chicken, coconut milk and galangal, the celebrated hot-and-sour shrimp soup *tom yum goong*, and *kaeng khio waan* (green curry), with chicken or beef, basil leaves and green aubergines. The intricate fruit and vegetable carvings seen at fine Thai restaurants are also a legacy of royal Thai cuisine. Stir-fries and noodle dishes are everywhere, due to the large Chinese presence in the central region.

Royal Thai recipes

The Grand Palace had many residences where each princess cooked what was called *ahaan chawang* (food for the palace people). These recipes spread through the wealthy classes via palace finishing schools and publications such as *Mae Krua Hua Baak*, the country's first cookbook, written by Thanpuying Pliang Pasonakorn, a descendant of King Rama II. The royal influence also spread to the wider populace through kitchen hands who had learned the recipes and started cooking them at home. A number of Thai restaurants connected to royalty began to open from the 1980s, but few authentic ones remain today. The intricate fruit-and-vegetable carving seen at fine Thai restaurants – such as the Sala Rim Naam at the Oriental Hotel – is also a legacy of Royal Thai cuisine.

Trays of food at Chatuchak market

COMMON DISHES

Kaeng

Usually translated as curry, *kaeng* covers a broad range, from thin soups to near-dry dishes like the northern *kaeng ho*. Many *kaeng* are made with coconut cream, such as the spicy red curry (*kaeng pet*) and *kaeng mussaman*, a rich, sweetish dish of Persian origin with meat, potatoes and onions.

Fish

Fish and seafood have featured prominently in Thai cooking since ancient times. *Haw mok talay* is mixed seafood in a curried coconut custard and steamed in a banana-leaf cup or coconut shell. Other delicious choices to try are *poo pat pong karee* (steamed chunks of crab in an egg-thickened curry sauce with crunchy spring onion) and *hoi malaeng poo op maw din* (mussels in their shells, steamed in a clay pot with lime juice and aromatic herbs).

Meat

Meat – usually chicken, pork or beef – is normally served cut into small pieces and cooked in all manner of styles, such as pork fried with garlic and black pepper *(muu thawd kratiam prik Thai)* or the sweet-and-sour *muu pad prio waan*, probably of Portuguese origin, brought to Thailand by Chinese immigrants. *Neua pad nam man hoi* is a mild, delicate dish of beef, fried with oyster sauce, spring onions and mushrooms.

Noodles and rice

Bangkok's ubiquitous noodle shops sell two types: *kuay tiaw*, made from rice flour, and *ba mee*, from wheat flour. Both can be ordered broad (*sen yai*), narrow (*sen lek*) or very narrow (*sen mee*), and with broth (*sai naam*) or without (*haeng*).

Common dishes are *kuay tiaw raad naa* (rice noodles flash-fried and topped with sliced meat and greens in a thick, mild sauce) and *paad thai* (narrow pan-fried rice noodles with egg, dried and fresh shrimp, spring onions, tofu, crushed peanuts and bean sprouts).

FOREIGN INFLUENCES

There have been foreign influences in Thai food for centuries. Even chilli is a Portuguese import.

Fusion food

Recent years have seen some European ingredients and cooking techniques integrated with Thai food, often initially in Italian-Thai blends, such as Thai-style spaghetti with anchovies and chilli, served at cafés like Greyhound (www.greyhoundcafe.co.th), which has several branches around the city.

Other modern Thai restaurants use non-traditional ingredients and serve their essentially Thai dishes Western-style. Three common dishes are salmon *laab*, lamb *massaman*, and foie gras with tamarind, of which there is an excellent version at Long Table (www.longtablebangkok.com). Another Michelin winner, Copen-

Sirocco, the world's highest al fresco restaurant

hagen's Kiin Kiin, also has an outlet here, Sra Bua (www.srabuabykiinkiin.com), serving modern inventions such as red-curry ice cream.

International cuisine

Other well represented Asian cuisines are Indian – including the excellent Gaggan (see page 109), which uses molecular techniques – Japanese (check out Zuma Bangkok, see page 111) and Chinese, a huge influence on Thai dining, particularly in the ubiquitous lunchtime noodle dishes. Mei Jeang (see page 101) and The China House (see page 114) are among the best upmarket Chinese restaurants.

There's also a clutch of places filling a gap in the market for decent food at mid-range prices. The French-owned chain Wine Connection (www.wineconnection.co.th) does bistro fare and wallet-friendly wines. Other mid-range picks are Quince, Smith, the Spanish Osito (see page 110) and the Mexican La Monita (see page 110). Bangkok's favourite Western food, though, is Italian, with around 100-plus outlets.

Thai-Chinese

Many ethnic Chinese in Thailand still speak the Teochew dialect of their southern Chinese ancestry, and most Chinese restaurants serve Teochew or Cantonese food. Especially famous are goose feet cooked in soy sauce, Peking duck, a wide variety of steamed and fried fish dishes, and the bite-sized lunch time snacks called dim sum.

DESSERTS

In Bangkok *khanom* (desserts) come in a bewildering variety, from light concoctions to little cakes. Generally light and elegant popular treats include *kluay buat chee* (banana slices in sweetened and salted warm coconut cream) and *kluay kaek* (bananas sliced lengthwise, dipped in coconut cream and rice flour, and deep-fried until crisp). And don't miss the heavenly *khao niao mamuand* (mango with sticky rice and coconut cream).

REFRESHMENTS

Thais drink locally brewed beers such as Singha, Kloster and the stronger Beer Chang. Foreign brands have been enhanced recently by American craft beers. The growing choice of wines is expensive, due to high taxes. Rice whisky brands Maekhong and Saeng Thip are popular, usually served with ice, soda and lime. Fresh fruit and ice drinks often get a splash of syrup (and salt), unless you request otherwise.

> ## Food and drink prices
>
> Throughout this book, price guide for a meal for one, excluding drinks and taxes:
>
> $$$$ = more than B1,500
> $$$ = B700–1,500
> $$ = B200–700
> $ = less than B200

Lacquerware boxes

SHOPPING

Bangkok is a retail destination for both spendthrifts and penny-pinchers. If you know where to look, just about anything is available, from traditional Thai pottery and handwoven silks to funky streetwear and designer goods.

In Bangkok you can sniff out an antique under the awnings of an outdoor market or pick up a Hermès handbag from a glitzy luxury mall. While imported items are expensive, locally produced wares are the opposite. And with most shops, malls and markets open daily from morning until night, you can easily shop 'til you drop.

TRADITIONAL PRODUCTS

Teakwood carvings come in the form of practical items such as breadboards and salad bowls, as well as more decorative trivets and statues of mythical gods, angels and elephants. Bronze statues of figures from classical drama make elegant decorations. Natural fibres woven into place mats, baskets and handbags also make great buys.

Lacquerware
Thai craftsmen excel at lacquerware, which is the art of overlaying wooden or bamboo items with glossy black lacquer, then adding artistic images painted in gold leaf. They are also supremely skilled at setting oyster shells in black lacquer backgrounds to create scenes of enchanting beauty.

Ceramics
Thais have been crafting pottery with finesse for over 5,000 years. While original antiques are rarities, most ceramics are still thrown along the same shapes and designs of their age-old counterparts. Among the best known are Sangkhalok ceramic plates from ancient Sukhothai, most notably with distinctive twin-fish design. Celadon is beautiful stoneware with a light jade-green or dark-brown glaze, and is used to make dinnerware, lamps and statuary.

Benjarong originated in China and was later developed by Thai artists. Its name describes its look: *benja* is Sanskrit for 'five', and *rong* means 'colour'. The five colours of Benjarong – red, blue, yellow, green and white – appear on delicate porcelain bowls, containers and decorative items.

Popular blue-and-white porcelain, which also originated in China, has been produced extensively in Thailand for centuries.

ANTIQUES

The centre of the city's antiques trade is River City (www.rivercity.co.th), with

Gaysorn Village   *Chatuchak Weekend Market*

an array of shops selling genuine antiques and lookalike objets d'art. Note that the authorities maintain strict control over the export of religious antiques; dealers are usually able to clear buyers' purchases by obtaining export permits and shipping them abroad.

GEMS AND JEWELLERY

Thailand mines its own rubies and sapphires around the east-coast city of Chantaburi, and also sells stones from Burma and Cambodia. Rubies range from pale to deep red; sapphires come in blue, green and yellow, as well as in the form most associated with Thailand – the star sapphire.

Be careful when shopping for gems and jewellery. One of Bangkok's most infamous scams involves touts telling tourists that a famous landmark, such as the Grand Palace, is closed and suggesting an alternative sight, a detour that often leads to a bogus gem deal. Buy only from reputable shops endorsed by the Tourism Authority of Thailand and the Thai Gem and Jewellery Traders Association. These shops carry the Jewel Fest logo and issue a certificate of authenticity that comes with a money-back guarantee.

WHERE TO SHOP

Malls
The main shopping areas converge around Thanon Rama I and Thanon Ploenchit and are linked by a covered raised walkway, which means you can walk from mall to mall without ever touching terra firma.

Just a stone's throw from Siam Square is the high-end Siam Centre and Siam Discovery Centre, as well as Mah Boon Krong (MBK), a multistorey bargain-hunter's heaven. Nearby is the gargantuan Siam Paragon mall, peppered with high-end boutiques, cafés, and even a Ferrari showroom.

Further down the road is the even bigger Central World mall, and across Ratchaprasong intersection, the luxury continues, with Gaysorn Plaza and Erawan Bangkok (both on Thanon Ploenchit near the Erawan Shrine). Central, which began life as a Chinatown family stall in the 1920s, picks up within 100 metres/yards with Cental Chidlom department store. Sales are common at all these places.

Markets
Reputed to be the world's biggest flea market, with some 10,000 stalls, Chatuchak Weekend Market (see page 70) is a must. The sheer variety of goods available is astounding. Patpong Night Market (see page 64), in the city's red light district, has clothes, watches, CDs and DVDs, among other stuff, much of it of dodgy origin. Also worth an early morning visit is the Damnoen Saduak Floating Market (see page 78).

Jazz at Saxophone

NIGHTLIFE

Many visitors' expectations of Bangkok nightlife extend no further than the much-hyped Patpong go-go bars. They may be surprised to find ping-pong balls play only a small part in a thriving, cosmopolitan entertainment scene.

Bangkok's nightlife ranks among the best in the world. The Thai affinity for *sanuk* (fun) sees bars and clubs offering everything from blues, house and hip hop to catwalks, clowns and art shows, often all on the same street. There is a growing indie scene, luxury hotels have jazzy cocktail lounges, and barn-like bars put on Thai-style country rock.

NIGHTLIFE ZONES

Bangkok has three designated nightlife zones: Thanon Silom, Thanon Ratchadaphisek and Royal City Avenue (RCA), in which venues with valid dance licences can stay open until 2am. The rest must (or should) close at 1am. The reality depends on the political and police agendas of the day. Bribery is rampant, and often these hours are flexible. Following a spate of police raids in the early 2000s, designed to curb drugs and under-age drinking, nearly all clubs now require you to show ID to prove you're over 20, whatever your age.

The Silom zone includes the Patpong red-light district and numerous pubs and restaurants, but few dance clubs outside Soi 2 and Soi 4. Thanon Ratch-adaphisek has some huge clubs as well as a clutch of smaller bars that attract young Thais. RCA has the most focused club scene, although mainly Thai, not least because some clubs charge foreigners entry but not locals.

Other vibrant nightlife areas include the backpacker enclave around Khao San Road, which is also a hangout for twentysomething Thais, and Sukhumvit, which has the largest concentration of nightlife in the city, from Soi 1 to trendy Soi 55 (Thonglor), and is home to Bangkok's famous Q Bar (see page 119).

VENUES

Most clubs have a cover charge, which usually includes a couple of drinks.

Nightclubs

Dance music in clubs runs a gamut from techno through hip-hop, deep house, jungle, Indian vibes and countless variations led by venues such as The Club at Koi, Q Bar and Demo. International DJs like Tiesto, Example and David Guetta have Bangkok on their tour schedules, adding to a confident posse of expat and local DJs.

Calypso Cabaret   *Playing takraw, or kick volleyball*

Live-music venues

Good live jazz and blues venues include The Living Room and Saxophone; axe-hero rock appears at RCA; and look out for promoters Dudesweet, who take indie bands to various venues around town. Brick Bar on Khao San Road stages rock, ska and reggae, while at the nearby Ad Here players turn up to jam in a place the size of a guitar case. Tawandang German Brewhouse has an impressive arty cabaret fusion with Thai and Western influences. The Thai country-music forms Luk thung (Child of the Rice Fields) and Morlam (Doctor of Rap) are performed in large venues on the outskirts of town. Shows often include ornately costumed theatrics, while the audience, primarily of migrant labour from Isaan, celebrates with spicy food and rice-based whisky.

Bars

High-fliers can sip fine champagne and cocktails at the rooftop Sky Bar (with jazz) and Distil (New York lounge sounds), both of which offer great views of the city, while 'Lo-sos' head for Cheap Charlie's – with its excessively quirky décor – on Sukhumvit Soi 50. For Guinness and hearty grub, go to one of the many British pubs around Thanon Silom or Thanon Sukhumvit.

Gay scene

The thriving gay scene is concentrated around Silom Sois 2 and 4, be it quiet drinking and dining at Sphinx, boozy cruising at Telephone Pub or hard dance at DJ Station. Soi 2 is exclusively gay, while Soi 4 is more of a free-for-all with street-side tables (see page 65).

KATOEY CABARET

The world-famous transsexual *(katoey)* cabaret revues feature sequined artistes who have gone through various stages of sex-change surgery, performing saucy lip-synching song-and-dance routines. New Calypso Cabaret (www.calypsocabaret.com) at Asiatique has shows twice nightly.

DANCE DRAMA

Classical masked dance theatre called *Khon* is staged at Sala Chalermkrung Theatre every weekend.

NIGHT-TIME SPORTS

Bangkok at night is not all booze and boogie. Sporty types go disco bowling to music and flashing lights at several alleys in the city, play night golf at various clubs, or race their friends at the indoor go-karting track on RCA.

Nobody who comes to Thailand should miss the frenzied Muay Thai kickboxing bouts accompanied by the wailing of traditional music, and animated betting on the outcome. New Lumphini Stadium out to the north on Thanon Ram Intra remains the best, but Dusit's Ratchadamnoen Stadium and Channel 7 Boxing Stadium near Chatuchak Market (see page 70) also have mainstream fighters.

Map depicting the city of Ayutthaya

HISTORY: KEY DATES

Following a series of bloody wars, Bangkok became the capital of Thailand in the 19th century. The city has survived colonial intrigue, coups, counter-coups and financial ruin to become the thriving metropolis it is today.

EARLY HISTORY

3,500BC Bronze Age culture thrives at Ban Chiang in what is now northeast Thailand.

800s–1200s The Thai (or Tai) migrate from China into northern Thailand.

c.1279–98 Fledgling state of Sukhothai, north of the area known as Syam, expands under King Ramkamhaeng into the beginnings of a nation.

1350 Ayutthaya supplants Sukhothai as the capital of the loosely formed, but growing, nation of Siam.

1767 Burmese armies destroy Ayutthaya. The new king, Taksin, makes his capital at Thonburi.

1782 Taksin executed. Chao Phraya Chakri (Rama I) establishes the Chakri dynasty and moves the capital across the river to Bangkok.

GROWTH OF SIAM

1851–68 King Mongkut (Rama IV) reforms laws and sets his people on a course towards modernisation.

1868–1910 Through diplomacy with Western nations, King Chulalongkorn (Rama V) helps Siam remain the only Southeast Asian nation not colonised. His modernisation includes the abolition of slavery.

1910–25 King Vajiravudh (Rama VI) promotes 'nationhood' and launches the current Thai flag.

1925–35 The reign of King Prajadhipok (Rama VII) is ended by a 1932 coup, in which he 'ceases to rule but continues to reign'.

1935 Ananda Mahidol (Rama VIII) is named king.

1939 Siam is renamed Thailand.

MODERN THAILAND

1946–72 King Ananda dies mysteriously in 1946 and is succeeded by his younger brother, King Bhumibol Adulyadej (Rama IX). The

Prayut Chan-o-cha

1950s sees many coups and military-backed governments.

1973–6 Many die in a civil uprising that topples Prime Minister Thanom Kittikachorn. A democratic government is elected. Military rule is re-established in 1976 after demonstrations and civilian deaths.

1976–92 A progressively softer, military-backed government fosters an elected government in 1988. Coups, starting in 1991, lead to street demonstrations and casualties in 1992. A new Democrat Party government is elected under Chuan Leekpai.

1995–7 Successive governments, largely seen as weak and corrupt, end with an economic crash and currency devaluation in 1997.

21ST-CENTURY THAILAND

2001 Billionaire businessman Thaksin Shinawatra and his Thai Rak Thai (Thais Love Thais) party win power.

2006 Demonstrators with yellow shirts march to show allegiance to the monarchy. The army stages a bloodless coup.

2008 Thaksin, found guilty of corruption, flees the country. 'Yellow Shirt' demonstrators occupy Government House and Suvarnabhumi Airport. The courts disband the ruling political party, instating the Democrat Party.

2009 Pro-Thaksin UDD protestors (Red Shirts) disrupt the ASEAN Summit in Pattaya; Songkran riots erupt in Bangkok; Yellow Shirt leader Sondhi Limthongkul is shot, but survives.

2010 Thousands of Red Shirt demonstrators occupy parts of Bangkok, clashing violently with the army on 10 April and 19 May.

2011 Thaksin's proxy Pheu Thai Party, led by his sister Yingluck, wins a landslide election victory.

2014 Coup d'état. General Prayut Chan-o-cha establishes a military junta, the National Council for Peace and Order (NCPO) and is appointed by the king to govern the nation. The army arrests Yingluck, dissolves the Senate and announces an interim constitution.

2016 King Bhumibol Adulyadej dies, having reigned for 70 years. His son Maha Vajiralongkorn ascends to the throne.

2017 King Maha Vajiralongkorn (Rama X) signs a new, military-drafted constitution.

2019 Prayuth Chan-o-cha's rule as prime minister, entering its sixth year, becomes democratic after he wins the first general election since the 2014 coup, although his party does not have a seat majority. King Vajiralongkorn is officially coronated in May.

BEST ROUTES

Wat Phra Kaew at dusk

RATTANAKOSIN

This once fortified island is the heart of Old Bangkok, with its extraordinary Grand Palace, the largest museum collection in Southeast Asia, a shrine that holds the city's spirit, and street scenes little changed in a century.

DISTANCE: 3.5km (2.25 miles)
TIME: A full day
START/END: Tha Chang
POINTS TO NOTE: Express boats only stop at certain piers (see page 131). This is a long route; be sure to set aside a couple of hours for the Grand Palace alone. Admission to it also includes access to Dusit Park (see page 49). The route is best tackled Wed–Fri if you want access to both the interior of the Grand Palace and the National Museum.

THA CHANG

Take an express boat to the pier called **Tha Chang**, which leads to a lovely little market square of 19th-century shophouses and food stalls. If you are hungry, you can eat in **raan aharn** (food shops) around the edge or under the frangipani trees, where old women in straw hats chew on *miang kham* – a snack of betel leaves filled with morsels like chopped shallots, dried shrimp and chilli. It is a scene that could be centuries old.

GRAND PALACE COMPLEX

Emerging from the square at the main road, turn right for **Sor Tor Lor** on the right, see ❶, while in front of you is the white-walled **Grand Palace complex** ❶ (Thanon Na Phra Lan; www.royalgrand palace.th; daily 8.30am–3.30pm; charge includes entry to Queen Sirikit Museum of Textiles). This houses Bangkok's two essential sites – the Grand Palace and Wat Phra Kaew – the former royal residence and the country's principal temple.

Cross the road and walk ahead along Thanon Na Phra Lan, where opposite is **Silpakorn University**, the country's premier art school and a string of small cafes, including **Krisa**, see ❷. After 100m/yds you reach the palace main gate (the second gate), where a sign proclaims: 'Do Not Trust Wily Strangers'. Take the advice and ignore the touts hovering outside, who will tell you the palace is closed but they know the perfect alternative (this will end in a visit to a gem shop where the tout gets a commission), and follow the crowds towards the stunning gold and twinkling glass facades. It is forbidden to

The bot that enshrines the Emerald Buddha

wear shorts, but you can hire trousers for a small fee.

Coins and decorations

The ticket booth is 100m/yds ahead. Next to it is the **Coins and Decorations Museum Ⓐ**, with exhibits dating from the 11th century such as 'bullet coins', seals and ceramic coins in the downstairs rooms. Upstairs are displays of splendid royal regalia, including crowns, gem-encrusted swords and robes, plus decorations and medals made of gold and precious stones.

WAT PHRA KAEW

Beyond the museum is the stunning **Wat Phra Kaew Ⓑ** (Temple of the Emerald Buddha), which, as the king's personal chapel, has no resident monks. On the left as you enter, the gold mosaic **Phra Si Rattana Chedi** is said to enshrine a piece of the Buddha's breastbone. Next in line are the **Phra Mondop** (Library), which contains the *Tripitaka* (holy Buddhist scriptures) inscribed on palm leaves, and the **Prasat Phra Thep Bidom** (Royal Pantheon), surrounded by half-human, half-bird gilded bronze figures called *kina-*

ree (female) and *kinara* (male). It contains statues of the first eight Chakri kings.

Behind the Phra Mondop is a detailed sandstone model of the Khmer temple Angkor Wat, in Cambodia. Along its northern edge is the **Viharn Yot Ⓒ** (Prayer Hall) that is flanked on the left by the **Ho Phra Nak** (Royal Mausoleum) and **Ho Phra Montien Tham** (Auxiliary Library) on the right. Opposite Viharn Yot is the first of the wat's 178 murals that recount the *Ramakien*, the Thai version of the Indian epic the *Ramayana*.

Emerald Buddha

The main draw for Thai visitors to Wat Phra Kaew is the **Emerald Buddha**, which,

Chakri Maha Prasat

despite standing a mere 66cm (26 inches) tall, is Thailand's most revered religious artefact. From the 15th century the statue was moved between monasteries in northern Thailand, then known as Lanna. In the 16th century Laotian King Chaichetta of Luang Prabang briefly ruled Lanna and took the Emerald Buddha with him when he returned to his homeland. It remained in Laos until King Rama I (who before he ascended the throne was a celebrated general known as Chao Phraya Chakri), recaptured it from Vientiane in 1778.

Located in the *bot* (ordination hall), the Buddha, which is actually made of jade, not emerald, sits high on a golden throne, overseen by a nine-tiered umbrella and representations of the sun and moon. Kings Rama I and III made robes for the Buddha to wear, one for each season. They were replaced in 1996 to celebrate the current king's Golden Jubilee. He personally presides over robe-changing ceremonies.

GRAND PALACE

From Wat Phra Kaew, go south into the compound of the **Grand Palace** (building interiors closed Sat–Sun). Until the early 20th century this city within a city included kings' and kings' wives' quarters, ceremonial buildings, military and civil wings, and a prison. Following the death of his brother King Rama VIII at the Grand Palace in 1946, the current king, Rama IX, moved to Chitralada Palace in Dusit.

The buildings are roughly arranged in four clusters. On the left is the **Borombhiman Hall**, built in 1903, now used as a guesthouse for visiting heads of state, and behind it the **Buddha Ratana Starn** (Chapel of the Crystal Buddha). To the right is the **Phra Maha Montien Group**, which is dominated by three structures, opening with the **Amarin Vinitchai Throne Hall**. Built in 1785, this holds the royal throne, with its nine-tiered white canopy, and boat-shaped altar. Beyond this hall is the **Paisal Taksin Hall**, where new monarchs are crowned; and further back is the **Chakraphat Phiman Hall**, which was the royal residence for the first three Chakri kings. New monarchs still spend their first night here as a symbol of accession.

Grand Palace Hall

The large building to the right of centre in the palace complex is the majestic **Chakri Maha Prasat ⓓ**, the centrepiece of the Chakri Group. This Italianate structure, crowned with three spires on its Thai-style roof, was completed in 1882 to commemorate Bangkok's first centenary. The interior also blends Thai and Western features, a common practice during the reign of the much-travelled King Rama V (1868–1910).

Dusit Maha Prasat

To the right of this is the Dusit Group, which is centred around the **Dusit Maha Prasat ⓔ**, a hall conceived by King Rama I as the place for his lying-in-state. He copied the exact dimensions of the Suriyamarin Throne Hall, which served the

Dusit Maha Prasat   _Detail, Wat Phra Kaew_

same purpose for the monarchs of Ayutthaya until its destruction in the 18th century. The Dusit Maha Prasat is still used as the final resting place of honoured royal family members before they are cremated in Sanam Luang (see page 32). Also here is the exquisite **Arporn Phimok Prasat** (Disrobing Pavilion).

WAT PHRA KAEW MUSEUM

North of the Dusit Hall is the **Wat Phra Kaew Museum** ⑤, with its decorative lacquer screens and Buddha statues made of crystal, silver, ivory and gold. In the southern room on the second floor are two scale models depicting the Grand Palace complex a century ago and as it looks today. A café to the right of the museum has lovely views from the veranda of the Dusit Maha Prasat.

QUEEN SIRIKIT MUSEUM OF TEXTILES

Before leaving, the building to the left of the main entrance is the **Queen Sirikit Museum of Textiles** ⑤, (www.qsmtthailand.org). It has four galleries showing traditional Thai textiles and items from the queen's personal collection of haute couture. It is possible to visit this museum

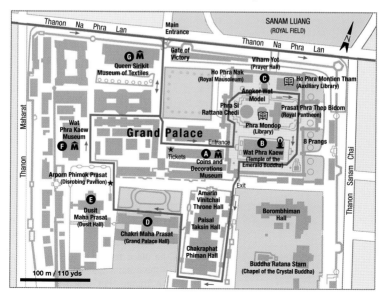

on its own for a lower fee, without admission to the Grand Palace Complex.

LAK MUANG

Leave the complex via the main entrance and turn right until you reach a roundabout with a central statue. Cross Thanon Sanam Chai and walk ahead to the white *prang* (Khmer-style tower) that holds the **Lak Muang ②** (City Pillar).

Thais believe everything has a spirit; religious structures are often built over the ruins of old ones in order to protect the spirit of the old. The Lak Muang is Bangkok's foundation stone, and is believed to contain the spirit of the city itself. It is seen as the point from which Bangkok's power emanates, and is the object of many people's prayers for favour in work, love or lottery winnings. The shrine contains two *lingam* (phallic columns associated with the Hindu god Shiva), the second one being the Lak Muang of Thonburi, which was moved here when the district (and former capital) became part of Bangkok.

City Pillar compound

On the other side of the entrance gate is a shrine holding statues of the city's five guardian spirits. Walk further into the compound; the nine Buddha figures on the right symbolise the days of the week, and night and day, each with a naked torch flame burning before it. People go to the combination that corresponds to their birth time and pour in bottles of oil, which represent life, to ensure long, happy days ahead. Opposite, devotees shake sticks from cups as another way of divining the future.

Near the gate at the end of the path, a **traditional theatre group** (daily 8.30am–4.30pm) performs scenes from the *Ramakien*, paid for by people whose wishes have been granted. Turn left at the gate into Thanon Na Hap Phoei.

SANAM LUANG

Recross the main road, turn right, and after 100 metres/yards walk through the large park. This expanse is **Sanam Luang ③**, where royal ceremonies and cremations are carried out. It was once a base for hawkers, fortune tellers and the homeless. Time will tell whether they will return. Each March the Thai Kite, Sport and Music Festival held here hosts fairground games, folk music and traditional sports.

NATIONAL MUSEUM

Come out of the park, cross Thanon Na Phra That and turn right. Make your way past **Thammasat University**, Thailand's second most prestigious educational establishment (after Chulalongkorn University), to the adjacent **National Museum ④** (4 Thanon Na Phra That; Wed–Sun 9am–4pm; guided tours in English available at 9.30am, Wed–Thu). Its collection, which is claimed to be the largest in Southeast Asia, and which was begun in 1874 with personal items belonging to King Rama IV, is displayed in

Buddha statues at Wat Yai Chai Mongkol

three groups in buildings that were once the palace of the deputy king (an office that was phased out in 1870). Galleries include those showcasing ancient Ban Chiang pottery, theatre, and the arts of Ayutthaya, Sukhothai and Lanna, as well as displays including golden royal funeral chariots, puppets and textiles.

Buddhaisawan Chapel

The **Buddhaisawan Chapel**, to the right of the ticket office, is significant for its beautiful murals and the bronze **Phra Buddha Sihing**, Thailand's second-most sacred religious image. The statue is paraded through the streets each year on the eve of Thai New Year, Songkran, the famous festival in which people playfully drench each other with water. Don't miss the **Walking Buddha**, whose pose is unique to Sukhothai art.

AMULET MARKET

Walk back along Thanon Na Phra That, take the first right into Thanon Phra Chan and then walk through the small market at the end leading to Tha Phra Chan. At the pier follow the left path into the **Amulet Market** ❺ (daily 9am–6pm), a busy warren of lanes where people bargain for all kinds of religious items. The lane running from the pier is lined with hole-in-the-wall cafés, where you can grab something tasty to eat (Mr Samaat's Roti-Mataba is a popular indoor place for pancakes stuffed with meat or vegetables). It leads eventually through Trok Wat Mahathat to Thanon Maharat. (Many of the lanes off it will also end here.)

WAT MAHATHAT

As you emerge from the market on Thanon Maharat, across the road is **Wat Mahathat** ❻, Thailand's first Buddhist university, whose name means 'Golden Relic'. King Rama IV spent many years here as a monk before ascending the throne in 1851. It has the largest *bot* in Thailand, with room for 1,000 devotees.

Head south along Thanon Maharat for 200m/yds to Tha Chang, where you can catch the express boat home.

Food and drink

❶ SOR TOR LOR

Royal Navy Club, Tha Chang; tel: 08 1257 5530; $

Part of the Royal Thai Navy Club but open to the public, this riverside operation is perched on a large wooden deck. It is recommended for fish and seafood standards such as spicy steamed snapper with Thai lime, curried crab and garlic prawns.

❷ KRISA

Thanon Na Phra Lan; tel: 0 2225 2680; $

This small shop is always busy with locals and does good Thai dishes such as green curry and pad thai, fruit juices and beers. Just what you need after a trek round the Grand Palace.

Boat on the Chao Phraya River

WAT ARUN & WAT PHO

This route takes in two of Bangkok's most important temples, the famous Mandarin Oriental Hotel, and links to the early international trading communities that clustered around the Old Customs House in the 19th century.

DISTANCE: 6.5km (4 miles)
TIME: A half day
START: Tha Tien pier
END: Mandarin Oriental Hotel
POINTS TO NOTE: This is an easy walk; the distance travelled is mostly by boat. The Grand Palace and Wat Phra Kaew (route 1) can be added to this route by turning right onto Thanon Maharat from Wat Pho (10 mins walk).

Explore this historic stretch of the Chao Phraya River by boat, stopping off to visit the best of what the southern part of Rattanakosin has to offer.

WAT ARUN

From Tha Tien, take the ferry across to **Wat Arun** ❶ (34 Thanon Arun Amarin; daily 7.30am–5.30pm). Also known as the Temple of Dawn, it is one of Bangkok's main attractions. The confusing nickname – the sun sets, not rises, behind the temple – dates to the time of King Taksin, who led the Siamese armies here in 1767

after their defeat by the Burmese in the siege of Ayutthaya. The king first viewed Wat Arun at dawn, and chose the area, Thonburi, as the new capital of Siam.

Taksin incorporated the temple – at that time called Wat Magog – into his palace compound. He renamed it Wat Jaeng (The Temple of Dawn) and housed the revered Emerald Buddha here. King Rama I later moved it to Wat Phra Kaew (see page 29), near the Grand Palace. Rama II (1809–24) changed the name to Wat Arunratchatharam, and Rama IV (1851–68) later chose the name Wat Arunratchawararam.

The temple today

After renovations by several of the Chakri kings, the main Khmer-style *prang* (spire) today stands at 79m (259ft). The four faces of the *prang* have statues depicting events in the Buddha's life and steep staircases offering pleasant views of the city. The main *prang* and four smaller ones in the courtyard are decorated with tiny porcelain shards shaped into flowers, a technique that arose in the Ayutthaya era using recycled pottery

Detail, Wat Arun   *Wat Arun*

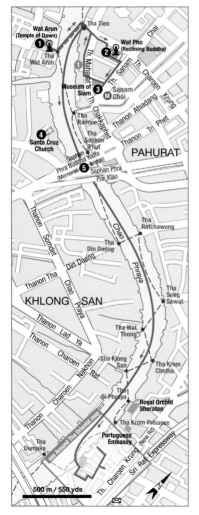

that had been smashed during merchant voyages from China. The trident of Shiva tops each *prang*. Other notable features include the 19th-century *bot* (ordination hall), in which the main Buddha statue contains relics of Rama II.

WAT PHO

Recross the river by ferry, walk past Tha Tien Market and across Thanon Maharat to the entrance of **Wat Pho ❷** (2 Thanon Sanam Chai; www.watpho.com; daily 8am–5pm). There has been a temple on this site for about 400 years, making it Bangkok's oldest. Following restorations and additions, it is now also the biggest. Although the official name is Wat Phra Chetuphon, it is still popularly known by a derivative of its original name Wat Photharam.

Reclining Buddha
Of particular interest is the enormous gilded **Reclining Buddha**, added to the site by Rama III (1824–51). The pose depicts the Buddha ascending into Nirvana, having reached enlightenment. At the far end of its 45m (147ft) length are 108 *laksana* (distinctive marks of a Buddha), rendered in intricate mother-of-pearl inlays on the soles of the feet.

Thai massage
In the courtyard are statues of ascetics demonstrating physical exercises, and on the walls a series of lessons on history, literature and astrology. Another legacy of

Santa Cruz Church

Rama III, they led to Wat Pho being known unofficially as the country's first 'university'. People still come here to learn meditation and traditional medicine, and Thai massage sessions are offered to the public for a small fee by trained practitioners.

MUSEUM OF SIAM

Leave Wat Pho by its eastern gate and then turn right. After 150m/yds, the **Museum of Siam** ❸ (4 Thanon Sanam Chai; Tue–Sun 10am–6pm) has interactive multimedia displays and tableaux explaining what it means to be 'Thai'. It starts 2,000 years ago and runs through historical eras and various population shifts, including the periods of Khmer, Sukhothai and Ayutthayan dominance. They also have temporary exhibitions on Thai culture.

CHINESE SHOPHOUSES

Take Soi Setthakan, west of the museum, walk to Thanon Maharat and turn right. After 50m/yds, on the left is a row of shophouses probably owned by the descendants of Chinese traders who originally set up here before Bangkok was the capital. In some cases, particularly the herbalists, they may even be selling the same goods. After 100m/yds, turn left down Soi Pratu Nokyung to **The Deck,** see ❶.

RIVER ATTRACTIONS

After lunch, go back to Tha Tien and catch an express boat towards Saphan Taksin. After a few minutes you will pass the cream-and-pink **Santa Cruz Church** ❹ on the right, which, although rebuilt several times, has been a place of worship for Portuguese settlers since the 17th century, an era when European missionaries, merchants and mercenaries all plied their trade along the Chao Phraya River up to Ayutthaya.

Further on are the black iron spans of **Memorial Bridge** ❺. Though the bridge wasn't built at the time, it was at a river crossing here that the mid-19th-century Scottish merchant Robert Hunter first saw the original Siamese twins, Chang and Eng, swimming near the bank. He arranged to send them to the US, where they appeared in P.T. Barnum's Circus.

Just after the Royal Orchid Sheraton, about 1km (0.6 miles) further down river on the left, a green-and-red flag marks the **Portuguese Embassy**.

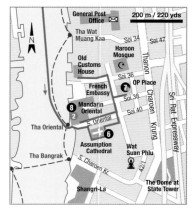

Reclining Buddha   *Riverside drinks at the Mandarin Oriental*

When it opened in the early 19th century, it was the first foreign embassy in Thailand. Further on the left, the crumbling white colonial building housing fire engines is the Old Customs House.

AROUND THA ORIENTAL

Alight at Tha Oriental. The lanes around here branch off Thanon Charoen Krung, which was Thailand's first paved road when it was built in 1861. It ran through Chinatown, turning this area into the main location for international businesses. It is now full of gold, silver and antiques shops.

From Tha Oriental, stroll past food stalls and the dilapidated Venetian-style buildings of the **East Asiatic Company** and the former **Chartered Bank**. Turn right under the archway after 50m/yds to enter a small square that contains **Assumption Cathedral** ❻ (23 Charoen Krung Soi 38; tel: 0 2234 8556; daily 6am–9pm). Its rococo interior incorporates an intricate altar, domed ceiling and stained-glass windows.

Leave the cathedral, walk down the side of the building and turn left at Assumption College. At the end of this alley, note the carved wood roofs on the old shops opposite, and take the small *soi* beside them on the left. At the top of this lane, opposite is **Haroon Mosque**, part of a Muslim community whose wooden houses have occupied this stretch of river since the 19th century.

Turn left and walk 100m/yds to the entrance of the **Old Customs House**.

This handsome though neglected building was known as the southern gate of the city in the 19th century.

Now go back the way you came, turn right at the French Embassy then left into **OP Place** ❼ (30/1 Charoen Krung Soi 38; tel: 0 2266 0186; daily 10am–7pm), which is billed as an Asian Heritage Shopping Centre.

Oriental Hotel

Turn left out of OP Place, then right on Soi 40, towards the river. On the right is the **Mandarin Oriental Bangkok** ❽ (see page 105), where rock stars might mingle with royalty in the jazz bar. Finish the tour with a break at its riverfront **Verandah**, see ❷.

Food and drink

❶ THE DECK

Arun Residence, 36–38 Soi Pratoo Nok Yoong; tel: 0 2221 9158; $$

Dishes up Thai-Euro fusion fare, such as carpaccio of tea-smoked duck, against a cute backdrop with outdoor seating, views of Wat Arun and a third-floor bar.

❷ THE VERANDAH

Mandarin Oriental Bangkok, 48 Charoen Krung Soi 40; tel: 0 2659 9000; $$$

Watch the boats from the terrace while you grab a coffee or dine on something more substantial. Smart-casual dress code after 6pm.

Royal Barge Museum

THONBURI

Take a boat ride along one of Bangkok's old canals to visit spectacular royal barges, the craftsmen of Ban Bu and a temple that was once an execution site in Thonburi, the former capital of Thailand. Then hit dry land for some gruesome forensic science at Siriraj Hospital and more savoury scenes at Siriraj Market.

DISTANCE: 6.5km (4 miles)
TIME: A half day
START: Tha Chang
END: Siriraj Market
POINTS TO NOTE: This route is mostly done by boat. The simplest way to organise this is to hire one from tour operators at Tha Chang. The pier is a good starting point because it is near the mouth of Khlong Bangkok Noi. Hire one for two hours, which will cost around B1,500 (cheaper if you bargain) and comfortably seat eight people. Arrange the stops you want to make before you fix the price and get in.

Nowadays, former capital Thonburi resembles cosmopolitan Bangkok's slightly old-fashioned relation. But this is a good thing, as its canals offer a glimpse of a fast-disappearing world in which most Bangkokians lived on water.

Canal life

The most common transport into the canals is the longtail boat, so named because it has an outboard motor on a 3m (10ft) pole angled into the water behind it. Sit towards the front for the quietest ride. Originally, people would come down to bathe and to pick up supplies from passing boats, which offered everything from food to a postal service. As you travel, small boats will pull alongside to offer you beer, bread or the energy drinks that are a staple of the Bangkok worker's diet. A little way upriver from Tha Chang, the boat will turn left into **Khlong Bangkok Noi**.

ROYAL BARGE MUSEUM

You soon arrive at the **Royal Barge Museum ❶** (Thanon Arun Amarin; daily 9am–5pm), which houses spectacular golden barges used on important royal occasions. Of the six barges displayed here, pride of place goes to *Suphannahongse* (Golden Swan), named after the mythical steed of the Hindu god Brahma. At 50m (164ft) long, it is the largest vessel in the world to be crafted from a single piece of wood. Barge pro-

Craftsman's forge at Ban Bu   *Longtail boats*

cessions date to the Ayutthaya period, but the original *Suphannahongse* was built in the reign of King Rama I (1782–1809). King Rama VI launched the current one in 1911.

Also on display are old figureheads, models of traditional canal transport, Ayutthaya-era drawings, photographs of barge construction, and gold ornamental cloths used to adorn the barges.

BAN BU VILLAGE

A few minutes by boat from the museum, there is a small landing on the left with stone steps and a short alley leading to the market community of **Ban Bu ❷**. The craftsmen here – the descendants of settlers who fled Ayutthaya after it was destroyed by the Burmese in 1767 – make bronzeware bowls called *khan long hin*, traditionally used to keep drinking water cool and to carry food to give as alms to monks. The village originally centred on small factory workshops that hired all the other families to do piecework from their own houses. Today **Jiam Sangsajja** (Charan Sanit Wong Soi 32; Mon–Fri 9am–5pm) is the only remaining factory. To find it, go left at the market, and after 70m/yds turn right into a gate in an unmarked brown fence (you should hear the hammering). They still make bowls largely in the traditional way by hand-beating bronze into various shapes and stone-polishing the bowls to a beautiful, deep lustre.

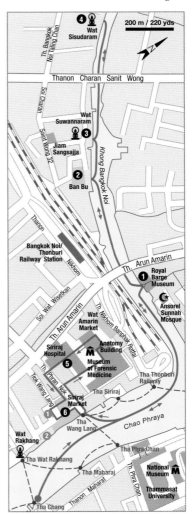

Wat Suwannaram

WAT SUWANNARAM

The next stop is **Wat Suwannaram** ❸ (33 Charan Sanit Wong Soi 32; daily 8am–4pm). This is a delightful temple, and because it is off the beaten track you may find yourself the only person there. It was founded in the Ayutthaya period as Wat Thong, and in the reign of King Taksin (1767–82) became the execution site for Burmese prisoners of war held at the nearby Bang Kaew Camp.

It was restored in the reign of King Rama I (1782–1809) and renamed Wat Suwannaram. Further restorations during the reign of King Rama III (1824–51) included murals in the *ubosot* (chapel) painted by contemporary master artists Thongyu and Kongpae, which are now the only surviving examples of their work. From the reigns of Rama III to Rama V the temple was used as a cremation ground for the royal family and high-ranking officials.

WAT SISUDARAM

A short way further up the canal, past verandas bright with orchids in hanging baskets, is **Wat Sisudaram** ❹ (Soi Sisudaram; daily 6am–8pm). From its pier, go right past the Chinese pagoda, where a man sells bread to feed fish called *pla sawai* which, in their hundreds, thrash around in anticipation in the canal.

A few metres further, turn left. There is a massage shop on the left and, opposite, a huge golden statue of **Phra Somdej Toh**, former abbot of Wat Rakang, located near the Siriraj Market. Before the statue are Buddhist and Hindu deities, and behind it, facing the river, a small shrine to Thailand's greatest poet, Sunthorn Phu (1786–1855), who studied here.

The red-painted wooden building across the courtyard from the massage shop is **Sala Kanparian**, a structure that dates from the Ayutthaya period and originally stood on stilts. The ground floor has now been built up with concrete. If you travel along Khlong Bangkok Noi on Saturday or Sunday you

---

History of Thonburi

Nearly 500 years ago the Chao Phraya River followed a loop through what is now Thonburi. In 1542 King Chairacha ordered a canal to be dug to cut off the loop and shorten the route to the capital, Ayutthaya. Over the next 200 years the canal widened through use and monsoon flooding until it became part of the river. The old loop was redesignated as two *khlongs* (canals), called Bangkok Noi and Bangkok Yai.

Bangkok, then called Bang Makok (Village of Wild Plums), was cut in two by the new river course. As there was already a fort on the western bank near Wat Arun, when King Taksin (1767–82) came to power after the fall of Ayutthaya to the Burmese, he chose Thonburi as the new capital of Thailand.

Deities at Wat Sisudaram   *Golden statue of Phra Somdej Toh*

can also visit Taling Chan Floating Market and see weekend trading as it used to be on the canals. Just ask at the pier to add it to your itinerary.

SIRIRAJ HOSPITAL

On the way back, ask the boatman to drop you off at Tha Wang Lang, also called Phran Nok, and walk from the pier straight into Thanon Phran Nok. After 50m/yds go through the gates of **Siriraj Hospital 5** (Thanon Phran Nok; museums: Mon–Sat 9am–noon, 1–4.30pm, times may vary) on the right.

King Rama V founded the hospital in 1888, and named it after one of his sons who had died of cholera. It was Thailand's first hospital and medical school and now contains a Museum of Thai Medicine with displays about traditional practices such as the use of herbs and Thai massage.

From the road walk 200m/yds and turn left at the **Anatomy Building**, where the first museums are situated. After this block turn right then left almost at the end. If you have a sturdy constitution, enter the **Adulyadejvikrom Building**, where photos of gruesome photographs on death and disease leave little to the imagination.

SIRIRAJ MARKET

Turn left from the Adulyadejvikrom Building and left again. After 200m/yds you are back on Thanon Phran Nok. Cross the road, turn left, and after 30m/yds turn into the alley on the right next to the chemist. Turn left at the top into Trok Wang Lang, the heart of **Siriraj Market 6**. Amid the clothes and general wares, this place is especially good for food. On the right next to a sign saying 'Wienna' is *som tam* seller **Pa Sidaa**, see ❶. If you turn right at the end of the lane, **Krua Rakang Thong**, see ❷, on the left, is a good place to eat by the river. Otherwise, turn left and take an express boat from Wang Lang to return to the city.

Food and drink

❶ PA SIDAA
112/5 Trok Wang Lang; tel: 0 2412 7189; daily 9am–7pm (closed alternate Sun); $
Serves grilled meats and Thai salads, but is famous for *som tam*, the fiery sour salad of green papaya laced with lime juice and chilli. It offers 11 versions, including the pungent Isaan original, with crushed black crabs and raw fermented sauce.

❷ KRUA RAKANG THONG
306 Soi Wat Rakhang, Th. Arun-Amarin, Sirirat; tel: 0 2848 9597; daily 11am–11pm; $
This old-style riverfront restaurant with views of Wat Arun is a good spot to dine on king prawns in sweet-and-sour tamarind sauce, spicy northeastern salads, and 'exploded' catfish, diced and fried until crumbly, then added to coconut soup.

Praying at Wat Saket

THE OLD CITY

Soak up the atmosphere of early Bangkok in lanes containing some of the capital's most important temples. For 200 years monks have shopped here for amulets, Buddha images and powerful phallic symbols.

DISTANCE: 4km (2.5 miles)
TIME: Five hours
START: Loha Prasat, Wat Ratchanatda
END: Phra Buddha Yodfa Monument
POINTS TO NOTE: To get to Wat Ratchanatda from downtown, take either a taxi or a river taxi along Klong Saen Saeb from Pratunam Pier. Tell the conductor you are going to Tha Saphan Pan Fah. The time given above does not include meal stops.

Together with the area covered in route 1, this part of the city comprises the spiritual and historical heart of Bangkok, with temples and shrines aplenty.

WAT RATCHANATDA

Begin the tour at the **Loha Prasat ❶** (Metal Palace; 2 Thanon Maha Chai; daily 8am–5pm), which is the most striking element of the **Wat Ratchanatda** temple complex. Rama III (1824–51) ordered the step pyra-mid-style construction in 1846, to be modelled on a Sri Lankan temple from the 3rd century BC. Its 37 black metal spires, each topped with an umbrel-la-like embellishment called a *hti*, represent the virtues needed to attain Buddhist enlightenment. You can climb a spiral staircase past corridors of meditation cells onto the roof, from where there are dizzying views.

In the wat forecourt, to the left as you enter from Thanon Maha Chai, monks wander around the **Wat Ratchanatda Buddha Centre**, a small market that specialises in prayer beads, Buddha images, amulets and pennants bearing the faces of revered monks.

WAT SAKET AND GOLDEN MOUNT

Come out of the wat onto Thanon Maha Chai and turn left. At the traffic lights turn right, go past the remaining walls of **Mahakan Fort**, part of the original city ramparts, and across the bridge. Turn right and cross the next bridge. A short way along on the left is **Wat Saket** (344 Thanon Chakkaphatdi Phong; daily

Metal alms bowls   *Wat Saket*

8am–4pm) and the **Golden Mount** ❷ (daily 8am–4pm).

This is the site of the former Wat Sakae, where King Rama I stayed and was blessed on his way to Thonburi to assume the throne in 1782. He later restored the temple and renamed it Wat Saket. Low-lying Bangkok got its then highest vantage point in 1865, when Rama IV completed the 78m (256ft) -high Golden Mount, so called because it is topped with a golden *chedi*.

Take the gentle climb past rock gardens with ringing temple bells and a 360-degree view of the city as the path spirals upwards. There's a refreshment stop halfway. The main temple complex of Wat Saket spreads out at the foot of the mount. The buildings include a seated Buddha and murals in the Phra Ubosoth (ordination hall), and a lovely wooden scripture library that dates to the time of Rama I.

MONK'S BOWL VILLAGE

Leaving the temple from the library turn right and walk 150m/yds to Thanon Chakkaphatdi Phong. Turn right, then right again at the traffic lights into Thanon Bamrung Muang. After 200m/yds go left into Soi Ban Baat, where the **Monk's Bowl Village** ❸ (daily 8am–6pm) is located, 50m/yds on the right.

Although you still see monks carrying metal alms bowls (*baat*), the bowls are now mainly machine-made, and there are just five families remaining of the original community that moved here from Ayutthaya in the 18th century to make hand-beaten bowls in the new capital. You can hear the alley before you see it – the noise of ham-

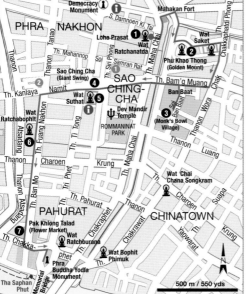

Buddha images at Wat Suthat

mers clack-clacking on metal as the craftsmen combine each bowl's eight metal pieces, which represent the eight spokes of the Buddhist Dharma Wheel, in turn signifying the Eightfold Path to the end of suffering. The bowls are finished with black lacquer and coloured inscriptions. It takes up to three days to make each one. You can buy them for between B500 and B1,000.

THANON BAMRUNG MUANG

Leaving the village, go back to Thanon Bamrung Muang and turn left. Cross both the small bridge and the main road (Thanon Maha Chai) and carry on straight ahead. The Old City is full of temples, and this street has typical shops selling accoutrements for Buddhist worship and funeral rites. It is not unusual to see pick-up trucks driving around with 4m (12ft) golden Buddha statues strapped to the back.

GIANT SWING

The square at the end of the road is dominated by the huge teak posts of the **Giant Swing** ❹ (Sao Ching Cha). Bangkok's original Giant Swing, erected by King Rama I in 1784, was based on one in Ayutthaya that had been brought to Thailand by Brahman priests in the 16th century. It was used to observe *Triyampawai*, the Brahmin New Year Ceremony, during which four young men in a gondola would swing ever higher, trying to catch purses of gold hanging from poles. The ceremony – a manifestation of a fable in which a serpent swinging between jujube trees tried to topple Shiva and cause the end of the world – was banned in 1931 after several accidents.

If you turn right at the square, on the next corner you will find **Kope Hya Tai Kee**, see ❶.

WAT SUTHAT

To the left of the Giant Swing is **Wat Suthat** ❺ (146 Thanon Bamrung Muang; daily 8.30am–9pm), said to have the city's tallest *bot* and also famous for its 8m (26ft) **Phra Sri Sakyamuni Buddha**, the city's largest and oldest cast-bronze Buddha. Its base contains the ashes of King Rama VIII. King Rama II is said to have helped carve the beautiful doors of the wat, which was begun in 1807, but only completed during the reign of King Rama III (1824–51).

Come out of Wat Suthat, turn left and go straight across the junction into the lane ahead. For a meal break, turn right then first left at the crossroads by the Siam Commercial Bank, and you will come to **Chote Chitr**, 20m/yds on your left, see ❷.

WAT RATCHABOPHIT

Head south where Thanon Kanlaya Namit intersects with Thanon Fuang

Inside Wat Ratchabophit

Nakhon. You will soon come to **Wat Ratchabophit** ⑥ (daily 8am–5pm), built in 1870 by Rama V. The *chedi* doors have inlaid mother-of-pearl insignia of the five royal ranks, and the architecture has both Thai and French influences, with outside decoration of *benjarong* (five-coloured ceramic) tiles and an interior that is akin to a miniature Gothic cathedral. This is typical of its period, which saw many official buildings mix Eastern and European styles. This square of buildings also houses a school and a cemetery for King Rama V's family.

FLOWER MARKET

Turn right from the wat and cross over the next junction to where the road becomes Thanon Ban Mo, with its bustle of hi-fi market vendors selling everything from mini DVD players to huge PA stacks.

Further along on the right is the beginning of the **Flower Market** ⑦ (Pak Khlong Talad), which continues into the covered area on the other side of Thanon Chakkaphet, spilling onto streets lined with displays of roses, carnations, sunflowers and myriad orchids. The market occupies a river location to receive flowers from Bangkok's outlying nurseries.

Phra Buddha Yodfa Monument

Turn left into Thanon Chakkaphet and after 100m/yds you come to Thanon Tri Phet. On the right, in a garden square, is the **Phra Buddha Yodfa Monument**, a seated statue of King Rama I erected in 1932 to honour Bangkok's 150th anniversary. From 7pm to 2am each night, the pavements around the monument come alive with Saphan Phut Market, operating from covered stalls and blankets on the ground. Among a wide selection of goods, the market is noted for clothing and accessories. Either take a taxi from here back to your hotel or walk south past the monument to the Memorial Bridge express boat stop.

Food and drink

❶ KOPE HYA TAI KEE

37 Thanon Siri Phong; tel: 0 2621 0828; daily 7am–8.30pm; $

This is a sweet Chinese corner shop with round marble tables and tasty noodle and rice dishes. Breakfast Set 1 (fried eggs with ground pork) is a favourite, along with fresh Thai coffee from the Chiang Mai hills.

❷ CHOTE CHITR

Thanon Praeng Phuton; tel: 0 2221 4082; Mon–Sat 11am–10pm; $

A five-table shophouse opened some 90 years ago by a doctor of traditional medicine. They have served excellent food (and medicines) ever since. Famed for wing-bean salad, *mee krob* and wonderful 'old-fashioned soup'.

Main Buddha image, Wat Benjamabophit

DUSIT

Leave the fumes of downtown Bangkok far behind as you take time out in Dusit. Visit a marble temple, paddle around the lake, then stroll among the gardens and palaces of Thailand's most revered king.

> **DISTANCE:** 2km (1.25 miles)
> **TIME:** A full day
> **START:** Wat Benjamabophit
> **END:** Royal Paraphernalia Museum
> **POINTS TO NOTE:** At the time of writing, this whole area was undergoing a large-scale redevelopment. Please double check with local tourism information when you arrive for up-to-date details. As much of this route includes former palaces and other royal buildings, appropriate dress is required: this means no shorts or sleeveless tops for men or women.

The royal enclave at Dusit is so influenced by European architecture, with its wide boulevards and neoclassical domes, that coming here is like entering another country.

WAT BENJAMABOPHIT

Built in 1900 during the reign of Rama V (King Chulalongkorn), **Wat Benjamabophit** ❶ (69 Thanon Rama V;

daily 8am–5pm) is the last major temple to have been erected in Bangkok. It has many distinctive elements, including a manicured garden courtyard with carved stone bridges over

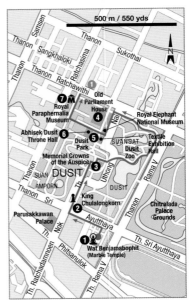

Wat Benjamabophit's exterior

a canal. The *viharn* (prayer hall) is designed in cruciform shape, with an exterior of Italian Carrara marble (the wat is also known as the Marble Temple). The stained-glass windows depict praying angels, a radical departure from tradition in material and subject.

The main Buddha image, containing King Rama V's ashes buried in its base, is a copy of the famed Phra Buddha Jinnarat in the northern town of Phitsanulok, which is said to have wept tears of blood when the town was overrun by Ayutthaya in the 14th century.

KING CHULALONGKORN MONUMENT

Turn left from Wat Benjamabophit along Thanon Sri Ayutthaya. Then turn right at the intersection with Thanon Ratchadamnoen Nok, where **Royal Plaza** is home to the equestrian **King Chulalongkorn Monument ❷**. People gather here regularly, but particularly on 23 October, the anniversary of the king's death, to give offerings and wish for luck for themselves in health, business and love. The offerings will often include brandy, whisky or cigars, which the king particularly enjoyed. Royal Plaza also hosts ceremonial occasions such as the Trooping of the Colour on 3 December, when the Royal Guards ceremoniously swear allegiance to the royal family.

THRONE HALL

Beyond the statue is the **Ananta Samakhom** (Royal Throne Hall; Thanon Uthong Nai), whose construction was begun in 1907 by King Rama V. It was finished during the reign of the next king. This building was closed to the public in 2018, but can still be viewed from the **Memorial Crowns of the Auspice ❸** monument.

King Chulalongkorn

King Chulalongkorn (Rama V) is so revered in Thailand that his photograph is still widely displayed in homes and places of work. He ascended the throne aged 15 in 1868, under the initial guidance of a regent, and is often credited with warding off the attentions of Britain and France, through clever diplomacy: Siam was the only Southeast Asian nation not to be colonised. After his travels to Europe and to Asian countries that had been colonised, Chulalongkorn returned with many ideas that helped modernise Siam. Regarding education, he said: 'All of our subjects, from our royal children down to the lowest commoners, will have the same opportunity to study.' He also abolished slavery in 1905, centralised government, introduced mapping and the postal service, and remodelled the judiciary, medical and banking systems.

View across the lake

Architecturally, this part of Dusit is intrinsically linked to King Rama V, who visited all the major European powers of his time and did much to modernise and internationalise the country. The king used the Champs-Elysées in Paris as the model for Thanon Ratchadamnoen Nok, which leads – in three sections – all the way from here to the Grand Palace in Rattanakosin.

The throne hall is a grand Italianate Renaissance structure with a domed ceiling and frescoes showing the lives of the king's Chakri-dynasty predecessors painted in 1911–14 by the Italian artist Galileo Chini. The building became Thai-land's first parliament after the end of absolute monarchy in 1932.

PARLIAMENT

From the Memorial Crowns of Auspice turn right onto Thanon Uthong Nai then turn left on Thanon Uthong Nai, which will bring you to Parliament and Dusit Park.

The **Old Parliament House ❹**, was the scene of several demonstrations between 2006 and 2010 by both supporters and opponents of former Prime Minister Thaksin Shinawatra. The blockades brought government to a stand-

The Old Parliament House of Thailand, a new parliament is being built along the river

Abhisek Dusit Throne Hall

still, on one occasion forcing MPs to flee over a hedge into Dusit Park.

The statue in the forecourt is of King Rama VII, who was monarch when constitutional government was introduced in 1932. Parliament has now relocated to Kiak Kai and sits on the bank of the Chao Phraya River.

DUSIT PARK

Beyond Parliament, turn right through the gate after the Elephant Museum to enter **Dusit Park ❺** (Thanon Ratchawithi; www.palaces.thai.net; daily 9.30am–4pm), home to several museums and former royal buildings. The following sites have also been sporadically closed to visitors lately, with no clear indication of when they will resume normal operating hours. Please check online or with tourist information before planning a trip.

The **Royal Elephant National Museum**, on the right of the entrance, occupies the former stables of the sacred white elephants, which, when found in the wild, automatically become the property of the king. The status of the white elephant is connected to the Buddha. His mother is said to have dreamt the night before his birth of a white elephant giving her a lotus flower, the symbol of purity and knowledge. A white elephant on a red background, designed by King Rama IV, was the emblem on the flag of Siam until the tricolour was adopted in 1917. The museum has displays of tusks and charms used by elephant handlers *(mahouts)*, photos and articles about elephant capture and training, and a tableau of the ceremony performed during the white elephant presentation. On the left is the **Textile Exhibition Hall**.

Abhisek Dusit Throne Hall

Across the lawn is the **Abhisek Dusit Throne Hall ❻**, which was erected in 1903 for King Rama V when he stayed at Vimanmek Mansion. The exterior has a beautiful mix of Victorian 'gingerbread' fretwork and Moorish por-

Abhisek Dusit Throne Hall

The Royal Elephant National Museum

ticoes. Inside are gold and silverware pieces and examples of nielloware, in which an amalgam of silver, copper and lead is used to add black detailing to carved silver and gold. The technique is commonly associated in Thailand with royalty or people of high office.

Royal Paraphernalia Museum

Leave the Abhisek Dusit Throne Hall from the entrance you came in and walk left then turn right and go straight ahead for 100m/yds. On the left is another display hall and, running around it, the wonderfully named **Royal Paraphernalia Museum 7**, which has exhibits such as antique palanquins, ceremonial gongs and Victorian hansom cabs that were made to order in London.

The gate ahead leads to Thanon Ratchawithi, where you can catch a taxi back to your hotel. Otherwise, cross the road and head right, then take the first left along Phichai Road for some food at **O.V. Kitchen**, see 1, or for more picturesque setting head to **Steve Café and Cuisine** on the river front, see 2.

Food and drink

1 O.V. KITCHEN

197 Phichai Road; tel: 0 2243 1980; Mon–Sat 10.30am–8pm; $
A clean, simple café serving up Thai dishes, including *kai pa lo*, a five spice stew with hard-boiled eggs and pork, and *gaeng garee* yellow curry with chicken. Check out the old photos on the walls of kings past and present.

2 STEVE CAFE AND CUISINE

Khet Dusit, Krung Thep Maha Nakhon; tel: 0 2281 0915; daily 11am–10.30pm; $$
Enjoy the relaxed ambience of this open-sided café situated alongside the Chao Phraya River. Feast on fresh traditional Thai dishes such as Tom Yam while boats calmly pass by on the water.

Giant Swing

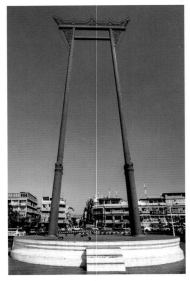

Ceremonial gate in Chinatown

CHINATOWN

Chinatown's boundaries stretch along the Chao Phraya, loosely from River City shopping complex to the edge of Pahurat Market. It is the centre of the gold trade and has a 200-year-old market, Taoist temples and a five-ton solid-gold Buddha at Wat Traimit.

DISTANCE: 2.75km (1.75 miles)
TIME: A full day
START: Wat Traimit
END: Pahurat Market
POINTS TO NOTE: You can get to Wat Traimit either by taxi or by metro to Hualamphong Station and then take a taxi.

Early Chinese traders had been coming through Bangkok since the Ayutthaya period, bringing luxury goods such as porcelain, which they exchanged mainly for rice. But Chinatown proper was established when King Taksin encouraged Teochew labourers and merchants to relocate from southern China in 1767, when he chose Thonburi as his new capital. King Rama I later moved the immigrants downstream when he claimed land to build the Grand Palace in 1872.

WAT TRAIMIT

Wat Traimit ❶ (661 Thanon Charoen Krung; daily 8am–5pm), also known as the Temple of the Golden Buddha, contains the world's largest solid-gold Buddha, a 5.5-ton, 3m (10ft) Sukhothai-era statue believed to date from the reign of King Ramkhamhaeng the Great (c.1279–98). On the left of the temple as you enter the grounds is a huge 600-million-baht marble *mondop* (pavilion) built to house the statue.

The *mondop* is also the location of the **Yaowarat Chinatown Heritage Centre** (Tue–Sun 8am–4.30pm), which explores Chinatown's beginnings through old photos, prints of period paintings and tableaux of old shop interiors. Once they had settled in Bangkok, many Chinese grew wealthy investing in rice mills, sawmills and *godowns* (warehouses). As their merchant influence grew, so did their access to the corridors of power through relationships with royalty and, later, politicians, who controlled the avenues to smooth trade. Today, many politicians, including former prime minister Thaksin Shinawatra, are Chinese-Thai. The museum's exhibits are well annotated, and it

Gold Buddha at Wat Traimit

makes an interesting sideshow to the Golden Buddha.

THANON YAOWARAT

Leaving the temple, turn right on Thanon Traimit and walk to the Odeon Circle with its Chinatown ceremonial arch. Turn right, passing the 'Golden Shine Foundation' with its Happy Buddha in the doorway, and the offices of the Chinese Clans Relations Cultural Centre, and cross Thanon Charoen Krung. Head northwest along Thanon Yaowarat.

Wat Tian Fah

On the left is **Wat Tian Fah ❷** (7am–5pm) and its hospital. Temples were traditional places of healing, where monks used many of the herbal treatments now popular in

spas. Wat Tian Fah has a 2.5m (8ft) golden statue of Guan Yin, Goddess of Mercy, who people pray to for recovery from illness.

Commercial hub

By the next corner you start to smell the aromas of Five Spice, that mix of star anise, cloves, cinnamon, fennel and Szechuan peppercorns so redolent of Chinese cooking. Shop signs are now in Chinese as well as Thai; restaurants advertise specialities such as bird's nest soup; windows proudly display whole sharks' fins (controversially, the fins are sliced off and the sharks thrown back live to sink to the bottom and die).

Look upwards at the buildings opposite for examples of 1930s Thai Art Deco. On the right, after crossing Thanon Song Sawat, look out for the

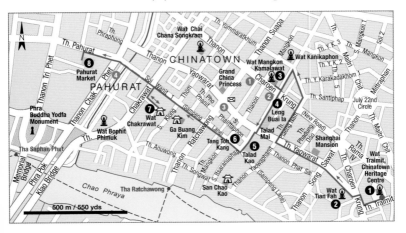

Temple roof detail

Tops supermarket. Above it sits the beautiful 1930s retro **Shanghai Mansion hotel** (see page 102).

Thanon Yaowarat is known as Thailand's 'Gold Street', and across the road you see the first of the large gold shops for which the area is as famous as for its food. Locals use the precious metal as emergency savings, buying and selling often to meet cash-flow demands. Dealers display the day's price, like bank exchange rates, in baat measures (1 baat = 15.2 grammes).

Cross Thanon Phadung Dao (where two famous seafood stalls, **Rut & Lek** and **T & K**, open for dinner at 4pm daily, until late), and then turn right at Thanon Plaeng Nam. Immediately on the left is a small store that sells masks and costumes for use in Chinese Opera and the Lion Dances that rattle and drum through the streets at Chinese New Year.

THANON PHLAPPHLACHAI

Wat Mangkon Metro station, part of the extended Blue Line, opened in late 2019. Cross Thanon Charoen Krung into Thanon Phlapphlachai and follow the road as it bends left. This street serves the many temples in the area with red-and-gold displays of paper temple banners and 3m (10ft) -tall incense sticks. The traders use paper with designs resembling banknotes to fold into various items that will be burnt as funeral offerings, a practice called *kong tek*. These are for the comfort of the deceased in their next life and include models of cars, houses and mobile phones. They also sell altars and spirit houses for use in ancestor worship.

TROK ITSARANUPHAP

At the end of the bend turn left into Thanon Yommaratkhum and left again, immediately, into Trok Itsaranuphap. This has more the feel of the original Chinatown, of hectic alleys and shops selling eclectic products. Old ladies beneath umbrellas are flanked by tangles of mysterious root vegetables and fresh fish in bamboo trays that they gut before your eyes and dispense wrapped in banana-leaf packets. Delicious deep-fried pork lies stacked in rounds like broken bike tyres. Beyond the food stalls there are clothes, crockery, trinkets, and more funerary items.

Wat Mangkon Kamalawat

Take a small detour by turning right at Thanon Charoen Krung to reach **Wat Mangkon Kamalawat** ❸ (daily 6am–6pm), which is Chinatown's biggest temple. Built in 1871, it is a place of worship for Mahayana Buddhists whose beliefs differ from those of the Thai Theravadist tradition. The building – originally named Wat Leng Noi Yee (Dragon Flower Temple) until changed by King Rama V – has Chinese and

Main altar inside Wat Mangkon Kamalawat

Tibetan inscriptions at the entrance, introducing a hallway display of fearsome Thao Chatulokaban (the four guardians of the world) in ornate warrior costumes. Along with Buddha images, there are statues inside of saintly figures, including one of the man who financed the temple building.

Leaving the temple, if you turn right along Thanon Charoen Krung, after 100m/yds you will spy the bustling **Hua Seng Hong Yaowaraj**, see ❶, on the left, which is a good place to eat.

To continue the tour turn left from the temple and cross the road into the continuation of Trok Itsaranuphap, which from here also adopts the name Charoen Krung Soi 16. Many streets in Bangkok have several names – old and new official names and sometimes even a third based on local usage associated with an area landmark. A short

Vegetarian Festival

Wat Mangkon Kamalawat is the centre point for an annual Vegetarian Festival, a Chinese Taoist event. For nine days at the start of the ninth lunar month (usually early October), participants wear white and abstain from meat, alcohol and sex. The festival area, between Thanon Yaowarat and Thanon Charoen Krung, becomes a sea of yellow flags, signifying participating restaurants and food stalls. Similar festivals are held nationwide at the same time.

way into the *soi* is **Hong Kong Noodle**, see ❷, an alternative lunch stop.

Leng Buai la

Another 30m/yds on the left brings you to the small courtyard of **Leng Buai la** ❹, which has a plaque inside dated 1685, making it the oldest Chinese shrine in Bangkok. The roof has glazed patterned tiles and a pair of stucco dragons, with dragon motifs also on the doorposts and inner pillars. The wooden interior is partly open to the elements and has a temple bell to the right of the altar that dates to the late 19th-century Qing dynasty.

Continuing down Itsaranuphap, the trays of fleshy black *ping talay* (sea cucumber), fresh meats, pastries and fruit mark an area called **Talad Mai** (New Market). Coming to Thanon Yaowarat, you could turn left and finish the walk back at the Odeon Circle, from where you can take a taxi home, or cross the street to the continuation of Itsaranuphap (by now called Yaowarat Soi 11). Here your nostrils are assailed by the tangy salt smells of preserved shrimp and squid, heralding the entrance on the left of **Talad Kao** ❺ (Old Market), which has been in business for 200 years.

SAMPENG LANE

Moving past the market, turn right at the alley crossing 150m/yds ahead into **Sampeng Lane** (also called Soi

Cooking noodles   *Chinese teashop*

Wanit 1), Chinatown's original thoroughfare in the late 18th century. The early Chinese immigrants toiled as labourers, rickshaw runners and dock workers at a time when the river was filled with wooden shops and houses floating on bamboo platforms. They ran two and three lines deep amid a constant clutter of trading vessels and cross-river traffic. By the turn of the 20th century, Sampeng Lane was notorious for its opium dens, gambling parlours and 'green-light' houses, the equivalent of Western red-light districts. The Lane was the trading ground for landlubbers, and though many of the wares will be new, many haven't changed since that time, and neither has the sense of chaos.

Dodging scooters laden with crates, you will pass stalls with dresses, bags, footwear, toys, party decorations, Thai flags, Chinese dice, sparkling acrylic bracelets and semi-precious stones for making your own jewellery. Most of it is available wholesale as well as retail.

Tang Toh Kang
At the junction of Soi Mangkon (or Sanjao Mai), on the right is the handsome facade of **Tang Toh Kang** ❻, the oldest goldsmith in Bangkok. Originally opened around 1880 further down Soi Mangkon, the business moved to these premises 90 years ago. It has a museum upstairs with gold items and examples of early crafting tools. On the opposite corner is a building from a similar period, once a gold shop, now a bank.

If you are tired after the next section of Sampeng Lane, you could turn left along Thanon Ratchawong and catch an express boat from Tha Ratchawong. Alternatively, you might be hungry now; if you turn right, and then right again at Thanon Yaowarat, you will come to **Shangrila Yaowarat**, see ❸.

WAT CHAKRAWAT

Moving on along Sampeng, the lane is now covered overhead and lined with fabric merchants. At the junction with Thanon Chakrawat, turn left and walk 100m/yds to the large stone gates beside the old Chinese herbalist and turn into **Wat Chakrawat** ❼ (8am–5pm). After 70m/yds go through the ornate gate on your left and turn right, where there is a grotto seemingly modelled on a cave temple, with alcoves for offerings, a mural and several statues. One of the latter is of a fat man; local legend says he was a very handsome monk who was pestered by women while deep in meditation. He responded by eating until he was so fat the women lost interest. The statue was built to honour his religious devotion.

Temple resident
Returning towards the gate, climb the small wall overlooking the tiny pond between two *prang* (spires), and see if you can spot the croc. People often take animals to wats to be cared for (see

Main entrance to Wat Chakrawat

page 83), and this one has been the recipient of several crocodiles over the years. The original – said to be a half-blind specimen called 'One-Eyed Guy' that terrorised the canals – is displayed in a glass case above the water.

BACK ON SAMPENG

Retrace your steps, turn left into Sampeng Lane and stroll past the stalls of beads, brocade, bangles and frills. The lane climbs a small humpbacked bridge over Khlong Ong Ang. If you turn left into the alley immediately after it you will find **Punjab Sweets and Restaurant**, see ❹, after 150m/yds. The aromas

are distinctly different here at the edge of Pahurat, Bangkok's Little India.

PAHURAT MARKET

At the end of Sampeng Lane, cross the road into Thanon Pahurat; 50m/yds on the left is **Kwan**, a small shop selling Thai classical and folk dance costumes and masks. At 100m/yds duck into **Pahurat Market** ❽ (9am–6pm) and root around in a two-floor emporium of all things Indian.

Catch a taxi home or go past the market and turn left at Thanon Tri Phet. After 15 minutes you will come to Memorial Bridge express boat pier.

Food and drink

❶ HUA SENG HONG YAOWARAJ

438 Charoen Krung Soi 14; tel: 0 2627 5029; $$

A busy air-conditioned café that sells all-day dim sum from an outside counter and all manner of congee, hot and sour soup, barbecued pork, fish maw and braised goose-web dishes inside.

❷ HONG KONG NOODLE

136/4 Trok Itsaranuphap; tel: 0 2623 1992; $

You will probably have to wait for a seat at this jammed alley shophouse, where cooks in constant motion ladle duck and pork onto noodles. Grab a custard tart at Hong Kong Dim Sum (no relation) next door for dessert.

❸ SHANGRILA YAOWARAT

306 Thanon Yaowarat; tel: 0 2224 5933; $$

The casual dim sum lunches here make way for the tablecloths and napkins at dinner. The menu then includes drunken chicken with jellyfish, smoked pigeon, and seafood from tanks on the ground floor.

❹ PUNJAB SWEETS AND RESTAURANT

436/5 Thanon Chak Phet; tel: 0 2222 6541; $

This small vegetarian café (also with dairy-free options) features South Indian curries, great-value *thalis* (a bit of everything), *dosas* (rice-flour pancakes) and Punjabi sweets wrapped in edible silver foil.

Floral offerings at the Erawan Shrine

PATHUMWAN

On this route you can drink snake's blood in Lumphini Park, dive with sharks at Sea Life Bangkok or blow all your money in the malls around Siam Square. It is not a day trip for the faint-hearted, although you will end in the serenity of the Jim Thompson House Museum.

DISTANCE: 4.5km (2.75 miles)
TIME: A full day
START: Lumphini Park
END: Ban Krua
POINTS TO NOTE: Start the route by taxi to the Lumphini Park gate on the corner of Thanon Rama IV and Thanon Ratchadamri, or ride a Skytrain to Sala Daeng, or the metro to Silom and cross Thanon Rama IV. This is a long route, but it is all close to public transport, so you can easily break off at any time.

The commercial heart of downtown Bangkok, Pathumwan is a sprawl of shopping malls. While it is mainly a consumer's paradise, there are still plenty of sights more reminiscent of an older and more traditional Bangkok.

LUMPHINI PARK

Bangkok has few green spaces, and even the biggest, **Lumphini Park ❶**, covering 58ha (142 acres), is relatively small. Enter by the southeastern gate,

unmistakable for its statue of Rama VI in the entrance square. This king owned the land when it was known as Saladaeng Field, until he donated it to the nation as a public park and fairground in 1925. He brought plants from around Thailand and renamed it Lumphini after the Buddha's birthplace in Nepal. The Chinese pagoda-like clock tower was built the same year. Nearby is the Lumphini Park Public Library, the first of its kind in Thailand.

Outdoor retreat

Until 9am the park is busy with weight-lifters, joggers and people practising martial arts on the grass before the sun gets too hot. You may also see pick-up games of *takraw*, a traditional sport similar to tennis, but played with the feet. Monitor lizards swim and roam around the edges of the artificial lake, where you can potter about in hired boats. The park is flecked with kite-fliers from February to April, and in the cool season, from December to March, it hosts open-air classical concerts every Sunday. You may come across a stall selling shots of

Shop 'til you drop at Siam Paragon

snake's blood, believed to be a general cure-all and aphrodisiac. Some 400m/yds west of the park is the Snake Farm (1871 Thanon Rama IV; www.redcross.or.th), with demonstrations of venom milking at 11am.

ERAWAN SHRINE

Come out of the park at any gate and hail a taxi to the **Erawan Shrine ②**. The three-headed elephant Erawan, which features in Hindu mythology, makes many appearances in Thai life, but the Erawan Shrine is actually dedicated to Brahma, the four-headed Hindu God of Creation.

It was erected in 1956 after an astrologer advised it would ward off the bad luck that was plaguing construction of the Erawan Hotel (now the Grand Hyatt Erawan), after which it was named. As the misfortune subsequently ceased, people believe the shrine has great powers, and it has become one of Bangkok's most visited.

Throughout the day people walking by or travelling in cars press their palms together to *wai* (see page 123) the shrine as they pass, and supplicants line up amid clouds of incense to buy garlands, joss sticks and other gifts as offerings in return for good fortune. Those whose wishes are granted might give thanks by paying the on-site dance troupe to perform.

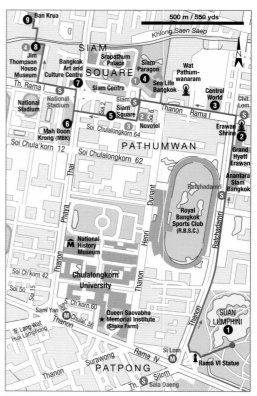

Feeding time at Sea Life Bangkok

SHOPPING STREET

From the shrine turn right onto Thanon Ploenchit and climb the stairs to Chit Lom Skytrain Station in order to access the overhead skywalk that runs beneath the tracks for several hundred metres in each direction. As this stretch contains many of the city's premier malls, it has been optimistically marketed as the city's Shopping Street, the answer to Singapore's Orchard Road. However, Bangkok's pavements are cluttered, crowded and uneven, so despite being featureless in itself, the skywalk does make movement between shops easier.

Central World

Turn left at the top of the stairs and after passing over the crossroads, turn right into **Central World ❸** (999/9 Thanon Rama I; www.centralworld.co.th), Bangkok's biggest shopping mall at 800,000 sq m (957,000 sq yds). It is owned by Central Group, a major Thai success story: having started as a humble Chinatown magazine shop in 1927, it now has over 200 stores throughout the country, with a turnover in excess of US $1.5 billion. In 1956 it was the first shop in Thailand to have fixed pricing. The mall is packed with high-street brands – fashion, sports, electronics, toys, cosmetics and restaurants.

In the cool season, the square outside Central World becomes a beer garden with rock bands and large-screen TVs, and is a major location for Bangkok's

New Year Countdown. Next to Central World is **Wat Pathum Wanaram**, a temple containing the ashes of the king's mother and his father, Prince Mahidol, who was the 69th child of King Rama V.

Siam Paragon

Leave Central World via the skywalk and turn right. After 400m/yds the path dog-legs to the left, ending at the Siam Skytrain Station concourse. Turn right over the walkway into **Siam Paragon ❹** (Thanon Rama I; www.siamparagon. co.th), another mega mall with cinemas, concert space and 250 stores.

Fashion takes up 30 percent of Bangkok's retail area, so it is no surprise that names like Cartier, Chanel and Jimmy Choo feature strongly, along with hip Thai labels such as Greyhound. Level four has Kinokunya, which is probably the city's best bookstore, while on level two you can walk among Ferraris and Lamborghinis displayed like dresses in shop windows.

On the ground level is a classy supermarket, a good wine shop and many restaurants, including **Taling Pling**, see ❶, as well as a good, cheap food court.

Siam Ocean World

In the Siam Paragon basement is **Sea Life Bangkok** (www.sealifebangkok. com), an underwater arena with 400 aquatic species displayed in seven zones. Highlights include giant spider crabs, cuddly water rats, otters and

Exercising in Lumphini Park

candiru, Amazonian blood-sucking fish that can swim into human orifices and drink their fill. Among local species on show is the archer fish, which spits spumes of water to bring down insects hovering above the surface. Farmers traditionally used them to keep pests from rice paddies.

Most spectacular is the transparent underwater tunnel allowing close-ups of all 300 sharks' teeth and bizarre face-to-face meetings with stingrays. There are regular animal-feeding displays, glass-bottomed-boat trips and diving with the sharks. A fun 4D ecological movie (the fourth D is sensory) has the audience -- both children and adults -- screaming with delight.

SIAM SQUARE

From Siam Paragon, go back to the Skytrain station concourse, cross to the other side and walk down the steps to the street. Carry straight on and turn into the first road on the left, Siam Square Soi 5. At the end, on the left, is the busy Isaan restaurant **Somtam Siam Square Soi 5**, see ❷.

Turn right into **Siam Square** ❺, a grid of *sois* that crosses land owned by Thailand's most prestigious educational institution, Chulalongkorn University, which is located on the southern edge of the square.

Unsurprisingly, the square is always packed with students and has a strong youth culture, including its own radio station with blaring street speakers that drown out the noise of the traffic.

For many years it was a hotbed of tyro fashion designers, and there are still pockets of boutique shops to drop into, but the sledgehammers have demolished most to make way for more malls.

Walk on -- turning left at Soi 9 if you want to stop off to eat at student-friendly **Inter Thai Food**, see ❸ -- and continue past the Hard Rock Café to the end of the road where you come to the vast edifice of MBK.

Sport of kings

Five hundred metres/yds from Siam Square is the Royal Bangkok Sports Club (1 Thanon Henri Dunant; tel: 0 2255 1420; www.rbsc.org), an elite members' hang-out that throws open its doors to the public every other Saturday for horse-race meetings. King Rama V donated the land specifically for this purpose in 1902, and some claim the royal charter is the chief reason why the sport retains its gambling licence despite some government opposition. Gambling is generally illegal in Thailand (along with racing, only Muay Thai boxing and the National Lottery are licensed), so only on-course betting is allowed; don't place bets with the illegal bookies outside. You can hire binoculars for a better view.

Mah Boon Krong   *Skytrain station*

MAH BOON KRONG

Beyond the mall turn left onto Thanon Phaya Thai. After 50m/yds climb the stairs over the footbridge to **Mah Boon Krong ❻** (MBK; 444 Thanon Phaya Thai). This huge old-school Thai mall retains a marketplace ambience, with stalls scattered around the floorspace between shops selling a vast array of goods, including cosmetics, cameras, phones, clothes and jewellery.

Art-lovers head for the ground floor, where teams of painters copy masters from Titian to Klimt for a few thousand baht apiece. The fourth floor has software and DVD stores; there is a food court on five; and the top level is dominated by a bowling alley, cinema and karaoke booths. MBK's market approach also means you can bargain at many stalls. It is always worth a try.

BANGKOK ART AND CULTURE CENTRE

Leave MBK via the Tokyu department store exit on the second floor to the National Stadium Skytrain station bridge. Walk straight ahead and cross the footbridge into the 11-storey **Bangkok Art and Culture Centre ❼** (939 Thanon Rama I; www.bacc.or.th). This space stages some of Bangkok's best art and multimedia shows, featuring both local and international artists and also has occasional live performances. Its retail outlets include independent galleries and organisations including the Thai Film Foundation and Bangkok Opera.

JIM THOMPSON HOUSE MUSEUM

From the gallery turn right onto Thanon Rama I. On the opposite side of the road is the **National Stadium**, venue for various sports, including football and athletics. After 200m/yds turn right into Soi Kasemsan 2 and walk to the end to find the **Jim Thompson House Museum ❽** (6 Soi Kasem San 2; www.jimthompsonhouse.com).

Jim Thompson was an American operative for the OSS, forerunner of the CIA, during World War II. In the latter stages of the war he served as an OSS station chief in Bangkok, and afterwards remained in Thailand. It was then that he spied the profitable potential of Thai silk; at the time the material was undervalued even in Thailand itself.

Clever marketing saw his fabrics used extensively in the 1956 film *The King & I*, starring Yul Brynner. The movie – banned in Thailand for disrespectful portrayal of the monarchy – was a major influence in securing an international market for Thai silk.

The former architect also appreciated traditional Thai houses and he transported several single rooms from upcountry to reconstruct them in Bangkok. Traditional Thai houses

Jim Thompson House Museum

are built without nails, which means that they can easily be taken down and relocated. On getting married, for instance, a groom would dismantle his room and attach it to his bride's family home, adding to the cluster of buildings in which extended families traditionally lived.

Thompson's house is a typical cluster arrangement, now rarely seen in Thailand. The collection of antiques inside is particularly strong on religious art and porcelain. Regular guided tours of the house take around 30 minutes.

Also in the grounds are top-quality silk and souvenir shops, and the minimalist **Jim Thompson Bar & Restaurant**, see ❹.

BAN KRUA

Thompson constructed his house opposite the canalside Muslim village of **Ban Krua** ❾. Its inhabitants were specialist silk weavers whose ancestors moved here from Cambodia in the 19th century. There are just two workshops still active, which you can visit by turning left from the Jim Thompson House Museum, then left again along the canal. After 150m/yds cross the bridge and walk on to a small lane on the right. Just along here, a handful of women at looms keep alive a traditional craft that captivated the world. In the second shop you may be lucky enough to catch owner Niphon Manuthas, who as a young boy knew Jim Thompson himself.

Food and drink

❶ TALING PLING

Ground Floor, Siam Paragon, Thanon Rama I; tel: 0 2129 4354; www.talingpling.com; $$
This stylish café-restaurant has a Westerner-friendly Thai menu (not too spicy) with dishes such as pad thai, green curry and *tom yum goong*.

❷ SOMTAM SIAM SQUARE SOI 5

392/2 Siam Square Soi 5; tel: 0 2251 4880; $
This modern Isaan restaurant prepares treats such as spicy salads, sticky rice and northeastern sausage. So popular there are cushions outside for people waiting.

❸ INTER THAI FOOD

432/1–2 Siam Square Soi 9; tel: 0 2251 4689; $
Popular student hang-out offering unusual dishes like spicy steamed shrimp in lemonade alongside more usual fare such as crispy fried catfish salad.

❹ JIM THOMPSON BAR & RESTAURANT

6 Soi Kasem San 2; tel: 0 2612 3601; http://jimthompsonrestaurant.com; $$
A very stylish setting is softened by plenty of silk cushions. There's a general Thai menu and a Western selection offering pasta, burgers and sandwiches.

View from Sky Bar

SILOM

After dark, Bangkok's business district bursts with a different kind of life. The bubble of night markets, elegant puppet theatre and the notorious go-go bars of Patpong are best seen after sunset cocktails with stupendous river views at The Dome.

DISTANCE: 2km (1.25 miles)
TIME: A half day
START: The Dome
END: Thanon Silom
POINTS TO NOTE: While this route is walkable, use the BTS Silom metro line to complete it faster, as it runs along roughly the same route. Smart-casual dress code is required at The Dome, so no shorts or sandals for men.

As the only official nightlife zone in the city centre, the top end of Thanon Silom offers guaranteed late-night drinking. With so many bars packed closely together, there is a friendly, festival-like bustle that makes it one of the most enjoyable areas of the city.

THE DOME

Start the tour with a breathtaking Bangkok panorama: take the elevator to **The Dome ❶** (63/F, State Tower, 1055/111 Thanon Silom; www.thedomebkk.com; daily 5pm–1am), a complex of restaurants and bars that sits atop the city's second-highest skyscraper, complete with Bangkok's highest balcony.

Sirocco and the Sky Bar

The original and most famous restaurant here is the five-star **Sirocco** (see page 116). If you want to dine here it is best to book ahead. However, many people come just to soak up the panorama with a couple of cocktails at the **Sky Bar**. It's not cheap, but it's not to be missed.

MAHA UMA DEVI TEMPLE

Continuing further along Thanon Silom, the lively Hindu **Maha Uma Devi Temple ❷** (Sri Maha Mariamman; daily 6am–8pm), on the corner of Soi Pan, is named after Shiva's consort, Uma Devi. It was established in the 1860s by the city's Tamil community, who maintain a strong presence in the area. It is known to Thais as Wat Khaek, meaning "guests' temple" (*khaek* is also a less welcoming term used by locals for people from the Indian Subcontinent). The temple and surrounding streets are

Patpong Night Market

particularly busy during the Navaratree Festival in September–October.

The temple's main attraction for non-worshippers is the 6-metre-high tower, every inch of which is carved and painted in bright colours, depicting various deities. Near the temple, the sensory experience continues at the small stalls selling incense and garlands of marigolds.

The web of streets south of Thanon Silom here are packed with interesting little points including **Sompong Thai Cooking School**, pretty cafes and numerous independent art galleries. **H Art Gallery** (www.hgallerybkk.com; Wed–Mon 9am–6pm) is worth a trip, showcasing contemporary Thai art installations inside a traditional old mansion house.

PATPONG

Continue on to **Patpong** ❸, which became one of Bangkok's first Western-oriented red-light areas when it opened in the 1960s to cater to US GIs on R&R from the Vietnam War. Despite the ongoing sex trade, its two *sois* – Patpong I and II – have become prime tourist attractions, enhanced by a busy night market that runs along Soi I.

Nevertheless, you will still be hassled by touts flashing menu cards with a list of notorious ping-pong acrobatics, and surprisingly these – along with ground floor go-go bars with girls pole dancing in bikinis – are also visited by some women tourists, who drop in for a peek at Bangkok's seamier side. If anything the seediness here seems to pique curiosity of travellers as much as it dissuades them from visiting.

Patpong night market

The night market here sells all manner of fake goods, including T-shirts, jeans, CDs, handbags and the notorious Rolex watches. Opening prices will start high, but be brave with your responses and you will be surprised by how easily – and how far – they come down.

The atmosphere is lively, with all walks of life – pimps, punters, ladyboys, and shoppers from every country imagi-

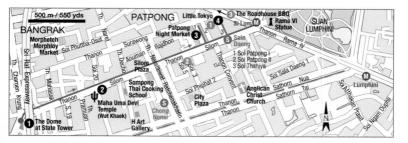

Tuk–tuk ride   *Night bazaar wares*

nable – and the tables outside bars are perfect for watching them all walk by. While Soi II has no market it does have the French bistro **Le Bouchon**, see ❶, and a 24-hour supermarket called Foodland, with a café and a chemist ideal for late-night emergency rations including noodles and aspirin.

SILOM NIGHTLIFE

You can end the tour at Patpong, but if you fancy a nightcap elsewhere, head back to Thanon Silom and turn left. The main road here contains the overspill of Patpong, with lots more stalls selling similar goods. After 50 m/yds, the small lane Silom Soi 4 is all bars and outdoor seating. There is a gentle gay scene here at places such as **Telephone Pub** and **Balcony** and a small club-bar called **Tapas Café**. On the corner is **Sunrise Tacos**, see ❷, and opposite is Soi Convent, with lots of restaurants and street stalls.

Little Tokyo
Further along Thanon Silom, Soi Thaniya is the city's **Little Tokyo** ❹, lined with sushi joints and karaoke bars, where hostesses stand outside greeting Japanese tourists with loud choruses of 'Irrashai Mase Dozo!' (Hello, welcome, please come in). In the middle on the left you may be lucky to see an illicit moonshine stall, discreetly placed beyond the entrance to a car park, where you can buy *ya dong* (pickled medicines) and possibly virility drinks

such as *Phaya Chang Sarn* (Power of the Great Elephant). Turn right at the end of Soi Thaniya for US pub food at **Roadhouse BBQ**, see ❸. Alternatively, there is a lounge bar, **White Rabbit**, if you turn left onto Thanon Silom from Soi Thaniya and walk 100m/yds.

Food and drink

❶ LE BOUCHON

37/17 Patpong Soi 2; tel: 0 2234 9109; http://lebouchonbangkok.com; Mon–Sat noon–3pm, daily 6.30–11pm; $$$
An atmospheric bistro with just seven tables, it is popular with local Francophiles for simple home cooking presented on a blackboard menu. Have an aperitif at the bar while you wait for a seat.

❷ SUNRISE TACOS

114/19-20 Silom Rd; tel: 0 2632 8588; www.sunrisetacos.com; daily 11am–2am; $$
All the usual Tex-Mex fare is here, including soft and crispy tacos and tequila. It does all-you-can-eat deals on some nights and breakfast specials from midnight.

❸ ROADHOUSE BBQ

942/1-4 Rama IV Rd; tel: 0 2236 8010; www.roadhousebarbecue.com; daily 11am–1am; $$
Spread over three floors, with bar sports on the top, this place does probably the best buffalo wings in town, plus US favourites such as burgers, BBQ ribs and apple pie.

Democracy Monument

BANGLAMPHU

After learning about the coup that toppled absolute monarchy at the Democracy Monument, stroll past Bangkok's oldest wooden building, take a riverside walk through Santichaiprakarn Park, and check out the nightlife on the Khao San Road, one of the hippest destinations in town.

DISTANCE: 3km (2 miles)
TIME: A half day
START: King Prajadhipok Museum
END: Khao San Road
POINTS TO NOTE: Khao San Road is at its liveliest in the evening, so this tour is best started around 2pm. To get to the King Prajadhipok Museum from downtown, hail a taxi or take a river taxi along Khlong Saen Saeb from Pratunam Pier to Tha Saphan Pan Fah.

Most visitors know of the Khao San Road as a famous backpacker enclave, but the scene is also enriched by young bohemian Thais, who help to make Banglamphu one of the most relaxed areas of the city, with a perpetual party atmosphere.

KING PRAJADHIPOK MUSEUM

Start the tour at the **King Prajadhipok Museum ❶** (2 Thanon Lan Luang; Tue–Sun 9am–4pm), and learn something of the intrigue behind the end of absolute monarchy in 1932, when Praja-

dhipok (Rama VII, 1925–35) was king. The museum examines the king's life through photos, official documents, personal effects and audio-visual displays. They cover his school days at Eton and his coronation, plus significant public works such as construction of Memorial Bridge. The king abdicated in 1935 and lived the rest of his life in England.

RATTANAKOSIN EXHIBITION HALL

From the museum, walk west on Thanon Ratchadamnoen Klang, crossing the bridge that has remnants of the walls of Mahakan Fort and Thanon Maha Chai. After 50m/yds is the **Rattanakosin Exhibition Hall ❷** (100 Thanon Ratchadamnoen Klang; www.nitasrattanakosin.com; Tue–Sun 10am–7pm). It displays the official history of the area from a mainly royal perspective, with multimedia displays including architecture, traditional arts and the Grand Palace.

DEMOCRACY MONUMENT

From the Exhibition Hall continue

Altar, Wat Bowoniwet   *Wat Bowoniwet's facade*

west for 100m/yds to the **Democracy Monument ③** in the centre of the road. Dedicated to the 1932 coup that led to constitutional monarchy, the central plinth, surrounded by four pillars, represents the country's first Constitution, protected by the army, navy, police and air force. The carving at the base was crafted by Italian sculptor Corrado Feroci, who adopted the name Silpa Bhirasi. He founded Silpakorn University and is known as the 'father of modern Thai art'. The monument was the rallying spot for demonstrations in 1973, 1976, 1992 and 2010 that led to many civilian deaths.

WAT BOWONIWET

Cross Thanon Ratchadamnoen Klang at the Democracy Monument into Thanon Dinso. At the end turn left into Thanon Phra Sumen, where **Wat Bowoniwet ④** (daily 8am–5pm) sits 50m/yds on the left. King Rama IX was ordained here in 1946, and King Rama IV was once the abbot. The interior is famous for murals painted by a monk called Krua In Khong, regarded as Thai-

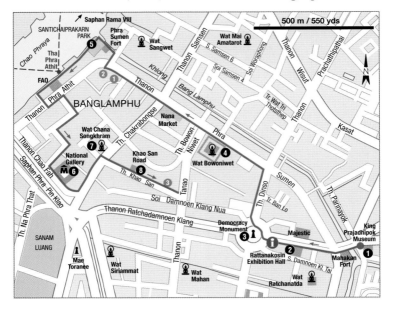

Thai Pavilion, Santichaiprakarn Park

land's first artist to work with perspective. The temple contains Thailand's second Buddhist University, along with Wat Mahathat (see page 33). Opposite the temple is Pratu Wang Kao, one of the old city gates.

PHRA SUMEN FORT

Continue along Thanon Phra Sumen and go straight over the crossroads into Thanon Phra Athit. You pass **Primavera Café** on the left, see ❶, and opposite, where the road bends to the left, is **Phra Sumen Fort**. Along with Mahakan Fort, it is all that remains of the 14 fortresses that protected Old Bangkok.

Just before it, trek a short way up the lane leading to a small bridge for a quick view of **Khlong Bang Lamphu**. This canal was dug by 10,000 Cambodian prisoners in 1783, during the reign of Rama I. It joined Khlong Ong Ang close to the Golden Mount to form the original city moat, called Khlong Rop Krung (Canal Surrounding the City). It is now disused, although you may see some monitor lizards hunting for food in the coffee-coloured waters. The dark plank structure on stilts to the right is believed to be the oldest wooden building in Bangkok. It was part of the original Wat Sam Chin, built in the Ayutthaya period. The wat was damaged by a fire that spread from a neighbouring noodle stall in 1869, and it was restored as Wat Sangwet.

SANTICHAIPRAKARN PARK

Return from the bridge and walk around the back of Phra Sumen Fort into the riverside **Santichaiprakarn Park** ❺, where there are good views of the impressive King Rama VIII Bridge. If you are hungry at this point, cross the road for **Roti-Mataba**, see ❷.

Follow the path past the Thai pavilion. In an enclosure at the water's edge are the six remaining *lamphu* trees that give the area its name, Bang Lamphu (Village of the Lamphu). The path snakes past the trees to the river front, taking you beyond the express boat stops at Tha Phra Athit and the United Nations **FAO** office. You can see the European-style buildings of the latter through the fence. The structure was originally the Maliwan Palace, home to generations of princes. In World War II it housed the operations rooms for the pro-Allies Seri Thai (Free Thai) Movement.

Towards Wat Chana Songkhram

A little further on is **Old Phra Athit Pier**, now a narrow bar-cum-café. Turn left here to Thanon Phra Athit. Cross the road, turn left, then right after 50m/yds into Soi Chana Songkhram, a short lane where the backpacker milieu begins in earnest with guesthouses, tailors, and travel agents offering cheap buses and flights to Chiang Mai and the islands.

At the end, turn right, then first left at the top, following the walls of Wat Chana Songkhram. After 100m/

Phra Sumen Fort

Khao San Road

yds you will reach **The National Gallery** (4 Thanon Chao Fa; Wed–Sun 9am–4pm), a meandering collection of buildings housing Thai artefacts, sculptures and art from various centuries.

Once you leave the National Gallery, turn left onto Thanon Chakrabongse.

WAT CHANA SONGKHRAM

Head a short way northeast along Thanon Chakrabongse for **Wat Chana Songkhram** (daily 8am–6pm) on the left. Ethnic Mon monks worshipped at this temple in its early years when it had a Mon name, Wat Tong Pu. In 1787 King Rama I prescribed the current name, meaning War Victory Temple, after his brother's success in the Battle of the Nine Armies against the Burmese.

KHAO SAN ROAD

Opposite the temple is **Khao San Road** , where homeowners first opened their doors to paying guests in 1982 during the Bangkok Bicentennial. The strip quickly became a legendary stopover for budget travellers on round-the-world trips and achieved wider fame after it featured in the book and film *The Beach* (2000) by Alex Garland and Danny Boyle respectively.

Nowadays, it is a mix of Eastern and Western twenty-something culture and one of the most vibrant areas of the city.

Walking from Thanon Chakrabongse, you pass jugglers, buskers, tattooists, hair-braiders, body-piercers, tarot readers, fish foot massages (best avoided) and dealers in fake IDs. There are well-stocked second-hand bookshops, wholesale silver merchants and women from northern hill tribes selling jewellery. Street-side bars tempt people to linger and watch the world go by, and there are also clubs, including the good live-music venue **Brick Bar**, see , at the end of the street on the left.

Food and drink

❶ PRIMAVERA

56 Th Phra Sumen; tel: 0 2281 4718; $$
Wood-panelled, European-style coffee shop. Top billing on a short menu goes to pizza, along with liver pâté and fried calamari. There's a reasonable choice of ice creams and coffees.

❷ ROTI-MATABA

136 Thanon Phra Athit; tel: 0 2282 2119; www.roti-mataba.net; Tue–Sun; $
Dip unleavened *roti* and meat-stuffed *mataba* breads into delicious *massaman* and korma curries of fish, vegetables or meat. Be prepared to queue.

❸ BRICK BAR

265 Khao San Road; tel: 0 2629 4556; www.brickbarkhaosan.com; $$
Brick Bar's stage hosts three bands a night, while the Thai and Western menu includes spicy salads, stir-fries and pizzas.

Religious items for sale

CHATUCHAK

Touted as the biggest flea market in the world, Chatuchak – or JJ, as local people call it – has pretty much anything you can imagine, from beads and Buddhas to snakes and violins.

DISTANCE: 1km (0.6 miles)
TIME: A half day
START: Kamphaeng Phet Station
END: Mo Chit Skytrain Station
POINTS TO NOTE: To get from downtown to the market take the metro to Kamphaeng Phet. Make the return journey by Skytrain from Mo Chit Station or by metro from Chatuchak Park; the stations are next to each other. The journey is about 20 minutes each way. The market is open from 8am–6pm on Saturdays and Sundays. Boxing takes place on Sunday afternoons.

Chatuchak Market has an estimated 10,000 stalls that attract 250,000 shoppers each weekend. Although the size and bustle of the main market makes navigation confusing, there is a logic to it. The stalls are arranged by themed zones in numbered blocks, each in a grid pattern criss-crossed by alleys called *sois* and *sub sois* (similar to the city's street system). Overhead signs indicate the section number, while addresses are marked above each stall and may read, for example, 23, 301, 4/1, corresponding to the section, stall number, *soi* and *sub soi*. Keep your valuables close by; as with any crowded place, there are pickpockets on the prowl.

A wider and mainly pedestrianised ring road offers a quick way to move between sections and breezier respite when the going gets tough and hot.

CERAMICS, PUPPETS AND ESSENTIAL OILS

Start the tour at Kamphaeng Phet Metro Station, and turn left onto the ring road past buskers that might include classical masked dance performers and people playing the Thai xylophone. Food-sellers along the right include **Funtalop**, see ❶, if you want a pit-stop or to soak up the scene before you dive in.

On the left are books, musical instruments and, at the end, wooden classical Thai statuary. On the opposite corner, beside the ceramics trader, take the alley immediately on the right (Soi 1), where a stall dispenses essential oils of lemongrass, orchid, lilac, vanilla and so

Market shopping   *Artistic wares*

on. Next door is a sandstone outlet with spa-like wall plaques and huge Buddha faces that might enrich your garden.

Past the next alley, a jumble of tapestries make a colourful backdrop for puppets hanging from threads. A few metres further on, **Lek Antiques** displays porcelain jars, fishbone chess sets and red-leather Chinese boxes.

BAGS, BLOUSES AND BEADS

Turn left into Soi 1/6, where the café-bar **Viva 8** serves coffee, tea and beer, with bands playing from 6pm as the market closes down. Carry on to the end, past scarves and shawls at **Rattanaporn**, and across Soi 2 into the alley opposite. A few metres down, long-haired Kai sells handmade satchels with original designs based on hill-tribe patterns, and ethnic jewellery from Tibet and Nepal.

Walk on and turn left at Soi 3. **Nayana**, on the right, has cotton shirts and blouses with mandarin collars and traditional Thai detailing. Next door is **Ta**, selling chains and beads of amethyst, buffalo bone and sea bamboo for making your own jewellery.

OPIUM WEIGHTS AND MASSAGE

Turn right here and right again at Soi 4. At the corner of Sub Soi 7 a musty stall sells bronze and copper bowls, temple bells, gongs and tiny animal-shaped opium weights from Burma. At the end of Soi 4, Chatuchak's **central square** is ringed by stalls mainly selling clothes, most of which are Thai sizes, and just down on the right there's a no-name massage stall where you can get relief for those aching feet from B150.

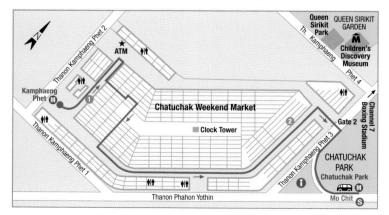

POP T-SHIRTS AND REVOLUTION

Across the square, in Section 23, Soi 32, a bunch of T-shirt stalls includes Japanese and superhero designs at Work, tucked down 32/6 on the left, and several easy-come-easy-go stalls with original motifs, from robots to romantic fantasy. At the corner of 31/3 on the left is **Red Star House**, where designer Kris sells revolutionary souvenirs.

COWBOYS AND FASHION

At the end of Soi 32 is the pedestrian ring road. Turn left, passing stalls loaded with hats, plants and trousers, and by the entrance to Section 21 you will see a drinks stand, known simply as **Shop Coke**. Perch here on a plastic stool and have a refreshing coconut juice directly from the shell. Beside Section 12 is **The Cowboy Shop**, recognisable by the wizened Thai hillbillies in Stetsons playing banjos outside.

Just by Section 8 is the small **Jeed-Jard** café, see ❷, and next door is **Ga Dee Nang** with cutesy tops and fishermen's trousers adorned with vintage Thai and Chinese designs.

Leave the market by Gate 2, turn right past the grilled seafood stalls, bear left at the fork, then left again at the main road. Mo Chit Skytrain Station is located just 150m/yds ahead, with Chatuchak Park MetroStation situated to the left.

THAI BOXING

For a chance to catch some live Thai boxing, head out the other side of Mo Chit station to **Channel 7 Boxing Stadium** (tel: 0 2495 7777; matches on Sun 12.30–4pm). The sport, although brutal – arms, elbows, knees and feet are all used – is highly ritualised, with the contestants initially performing a *wai kru* dance of respect for their trainers. A traditional Thai *pipat* band sits ringside accompanying the action with a wailing of pipes.

Many of the boxers will have started their careers at seven years old at village temple fairs, earning around B50 for their first fights. If they're good, within a few years they will be their family's breadwinner.

Food and drink

❶ FUNTALOP

Section 26, Chatuchak Market; $

This stall's wooden tables are jammed with people eating deep-fried chicken marinated with soy sauce, tamarind and pepper, and *som tam* (spicy green papaya salad). Tables are communal, so be prepared to smile and make friends.

❷ JEED-JARD

Section 8, Soi 17/1, Chatuchak Market; $

This small, clean café has lovely cooling fans and sells northeastern food including spicy pork sausage, fried chicken with fiery mango salad, and the region's preferred sticky rice.

Boat ride on the Chao Phraya River

NONTHABURI AND KO KRET

An hour's boat ride north of the city, near the riverside town of Nonthaburi, is a beautiful temple and a small community of Mon, who make exquisite pottery on an island with no cars.

DISTANCE: 20km (12.5 miles)
TIME: A leisurely day
START/END: Bangkok
POINTS TO NOTE: Start the route from any express boat pier. The journey takes about one hour. To reach Ko Kret, catch a river taxi from Nonthaburi to Pakret Pier, then take the ferry. Alternatively, Bangkok directly to Pakret by taxi costs about B200 including expressway tolls.

Having caught an express boat from downtown, disembark at the final pier, Nonthaburi (10km/6 miles north of Bangkok), and take a ferry across the river, where tuk tuks are lined up waiting for fares. Negotiate a price with the driver to take you to Wat Chaloem Phra Kiet, wait for you and bring you back to the pier; it should cost around B50.

WAT CHALOEM PHRA KIET

Five minutes away, **Wat Chaloem Phra Kiet** ❶ (Bang Sri Muang; daily 8.30am–5pm) sits behind ramparts that are a legacy of the fort built on the site in the reign of King Narai the Great (1656–88), the Ayutthaya period. King Rama III (1824–51) erected the wat, in part from the fort walls, to honour his mother and grandparents.

From the road, you enter by the back door. Pass through an ornamental garden to the beautiful *bot* (ordination hall), which is notable for a Chinese-earthenware mosaic roof designed as flowers in purple, red and gold. The floor is decorated with mirrored tiles, the wooden windows have gold-leaf paintings of bucolic scenes, and there is a large copper seated Buddha. Also in the compound are a tall white *chedi* and two *viharns* (prayer halls).

This is a river-front temple; pass through the gateway beside the *bot* and you will come to a compound of rain trees with refreshment stalls and twin wooden *salas* (open-walled pavilions) from which to enjoy the view.

Lunch

Return to the ferry boat pier and cross back over the river to Nonthaburi Pier.

Reclining Buddha...

If you walk to the street outside, there are clean toilets a short way to the left, and 100m/yds to the right is the floating **Rim Fung**, see 1, a good stop for lunch. Ahead of you is the market town of **Nonthaburi**, which is famous for its fruit. The durian is particularly notorious: the fruit's hard, spiky exterior hides creamy flesh with an aroma like a ripe sewer, making it one of the strangest food experiences on earth.

KO KRET

From Nonthaburi Pier catch a river taxi to Pakret (about a 20-minute journey); the half-size longtail boats make for a high-powered, exhilarating and bumpy ride. The return trip is around B800 per boat, but they seat eight, so you can cut the price by sharing with other people.

From here take a two-minute ferry ride to **Ko Kret**, a 4 sq km (1 sq mile) island created during the Ayutthaya period, when the Lat Kret Noe canal was built to shorten the journey to the old capital. It is populated by Mon, a people of Indo-Burmese origin, some of whom were given refuge here when they fled the kingdom of Pegu, in Burma, after the Burmese king Alaungpaya destroyed it in 1757.

A single road, running in a loop around the island, links seven small communities, which although largely assimilated into Thai culture retain aspects of the Mon way of life. This, and the tranquil rural atmosphere, has made the island

a regular destination for Thai tourists, especially at weekends.

Wat Poramaiyikawat

The ferry stops beside **Wat Poramaiyikawat** 2 (Moo 7; Mon–Fri 1–4pm, Sat–Sun 9am–5pm), which contains a full set of Mon-language Buddhist *Tripitaka* (scriptures), given to the temple by King Rama V. Mon is still studied by monks at the temple, which is possibly

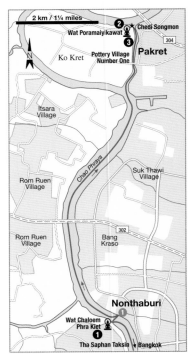

...in Wat Poramaiyikawat

Mon pottery in Ko Kret

the only place on the island where the language is still spoken.

A small **museum** displays old accoutrements of monastic life, including amulets and a *hem* (monk's coffin), as well as the bed of Rama III's daughter, Princess Lamom, which was donated to the temple after her death.

The temple sits in a small **park**, where families picnic under the trees; at weekends you can buy food at the temple market. In a corner is a white stupa called **Chedi Songmon**, which, due to subsidence, leans precariously towards the river. Local legend says that when it eventually falls the local Mon will be able to return to their homeland.

Food stalls

From the temple, head along the road leading south. Almost immediately you will pass food stalls beside the river, a good place to have a break for a drink or a meal of Mon specialities including *khao chae* (a bowl of savoury morsels served with chilled, jasmine-infused rice). This is now a traditional Thai dish, popular in up-market hotels, and eaten mainly as a summer delicacy.

Pottery Village Number One

About 500m/yds from the food stalls is **Pottery Village Number One** ❸ (Moo 1; daily 8am–5pm, workshop weekdays only). Ko Kret is best-known for its Mon pottery, which is intricately designed, unglazed and coloured orange or blackish-grey. The pottery village still has its

old-fashioned brick kilns (now superseded by modern ovens), although the traditional method of softening the clay – by using buffaloes to trample it – has been replaced by kneading machines. On weekdays you can see all the processes in action, from clay-slicing to carving. A shop sells items such as bowls, incense burners and ornate vases, priced between 100 and several thousand baht. You can also visit a small orchard on the property.

Touring the whole island takes about three hours on foot or half that by bike (B40 a day to hire at various points; motorbike taxis and boats cost B20 to hop between piers). It is a satisfying rural escapade, but the pattern of life – temples, orchards and pottery workshops – remains the same, so this is a good place to turn back if you are tired.

Take the ferry back to your river taxi, which will return you to Nonthaburi Pier from where you can catch an express boat back to Bangkok.

Food and drink

① RIM FUNG

235/2 Thanon Pracharat, Nonthaburi; tel: 0 2525 1742; daily 11am–10pm; $
Wooden floating restaurant with a menu including marinated hot-plate chicken, whole catfish and fried frogs, served with spicy salads. Thai country music accompanies your meal.

Phra Pathom Chedi

WEST OF BANGKOK

The countryside west of the capital teems with historical sights, from the country's oldest city and the world's largest Buddhist monument to fascinating ceramic workshops and traditional floating markets.

> **DISTANCE:** 200km (126 miles)
> **TIME:** One or two days
> **START/END:** Bangkok
> **POINTS TO NOTE:** Although the points on this route are accessible by public transport, it is a fiddly journey, so it is best to hire a car. Leave Bangkok along Highway 4, which starts on the west side of town at the King Taksin Monument in Thonburi. Stay overnight at the Baan Sukchoke Country Resort (see page 106), unless you can manage leaving Bangkok by 6.30am to catch the Floating Market at its best.

Once you get past the city's main suburbs, life west of the capital slows to a rural pace, with people tending the orchards and farms that supply Bangkok with fruit, flowers and vegetables.

SAMPRAN RIVERSIDE

After about an hour's drive from Bangkok you see signs on the left for **Sampran Riverside ❶** (Km 32, Thanon Phetkasem; www.sampranriverside.com; daily 8am–5pm). The 28-hectare (70-acre) grounds are nestled in an elbow of the Nakornchaisri River and are popular with families at weekends. There are herb gardens, mahogany, banana and flame trees, and flower beds with resplendent orchids and rare species. The owners have rebuilt antique wooden houses moved from upcountry and set around a lake.

Two daily cultural shows include morning demonstrations of Thai boxing, rice farming, traditional cooking and even elephant training. In the afternoon there is folk dancing and music. There are also restaurants and a hotel on site, if you want to linger.

NAKHON PATHOM

Come out of the Sampran Riverside and head west along Highway 4 for 20km (12 miles), then follow signs to **Nakhon Pathom**, which is popularly referred to as Thailand's oldest city.

Gold leaf offerings, Phra Pathom Chedi

Phra Pathom Chedi

Drive along Thanon Tesa, and after 2km (1.25 miles) the town's most noteworthy site, **Phra Pathom Chedi** ❷ (Thanon Khwa Phra; daily 6am–6pm), looms into view – at 127m (417ft) it is the tallest Buddhist monument in the world. At the end of the road turn left, then right at the lights and into the main entrance of the *chedi* on the right.

Indian-style Buddhist artefacts found here have been used to date the site to around 150BC, and conjecture that the city was the capital of ancient lands known as Suvarnabhum. Later, from the 6th–11th centuries, Nakhon Pathom was the centre of Dvaravati, an affiliation of city-states in what is now western Thailand, populated by ethnic Mon, with Nakhon Pathom at its centre.

There has been a *chedi* on this site since the 6th century, although the original was devastated in a Burmese attack in 1057 and lay in ruins until Rama IV built a new one over the remains in 1860. He constructed a replica of the original a few metres to the south.

The temple that surrounds the *chedi* is one of the most important in Thailand. It has four *viharns* (prayer halls) marking the cardinal compass points, each with a Buddha image. The northernmost, containing a standing Buddha, holds the ashes of Rama VI (1910–25). Leading off the corridors directly around the *chedi* are classrooms for novice monks, while the outer terraces are notable for Chinese statuary and a large reclining Buddha.

You can buy lunch at the **Chedi Square food stalls**, see ❶. This space is also used for traditional dance performances, and in an adjacent park each November people celebrate the end of the rainy season during the Loy Krathong festival.

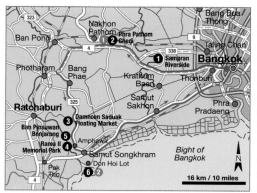

Chedi Museum

The **Phra Pathom Chedi National Museum** (Wed–Sun 9am–4pm), located on the edge of the square to the right of the *chedi*, has the remains of Buddha images and stone carvings from the Dvaravati period.

Overnight stop

Leaving the *chedi*, turn right along Thanon Khwa

Damnoen Saduak Floating Market

Phra, then left at the lights, opposite Silpakorn University. At the top turn right on Highway 4, and stay on this road following signs for Ratchaburi (Ratburi) for 17km (10 miles) before turning left (south) on Route 325 towards Damnoen Saduak, which is about 25km (15 miles) away.

After 22km (13 miles) look for signs on the right for **Baan Sukchoke Country Resort** (see page 106), a good place to spend the night. In the morning, to get to the market, turn right and drive for 2km (1.25 miles) into town.

FLOATING MARKET

The area southwest of Bangkok is laced with rivers and canals, and the surrounding countryside bursts with produce grown on farmland and in orchards. Traditionally, smallholders would take their wares by boat to local floating markets and sell them directly, while still bobbing on the water. The canal networks ran all the way to Bangkok, and you can still travel the full distance to the capital in this way today.

Over the last 30 years, however, roads have superseded waterways, the few remaining markets have become tourist attractions, and the traders, in their wide-brimmed hats, are poster girls for ad campaigns. That said, if you get to the most famous floating market at **Damnoen Saduak** ❸ before 9am when the tour coaches arrive, this is still a fun and largely faithful dip into traditional Thai culture.

Exploring the market

As you reach Damnoen Saduak go over the flyover, then turn right at the lights under the ornate Thai-style gateway into the small lane leading to the market. You can drive along it all the way to the bridge and view proceedings from dry land, but far more pleasant is to stop at one of the tour operators advertised at the roadside, where for about B300 an hour you can hire a boat for six people.

Every day the main market mostly sells foodstuffs, such as fruit, spices, vegetables and one-plate dishes cooked on board the boats, although around a corner a **second canal section** has handicrafts, trinkets, T-shirts and other souvenirs. Haggling is expected.

RAMA II MEMORIAL PARK

Leave town by turning right (south) onto Route 325 for about 10km (6 miles), then turn right towards the village of **Amphawa**, which has its own floating market (Fri–Sun pm only). Go over the bridge, then just after the large white temple turn left into **Rama II Memorial Park** ❹ (Thanon Mae Klong Bang Nok Kwaek; daily 8.30am–5pm). As well as botanical gardens, the park has traditional Thai buildings housing an ethnological museum depicting early Rattanakosin-period lifestyles and a display

Smallholders sell their wares from boats

of musical instruments. A fair here every February celebrates Thai music, dance and drama.

BENJARONG WORKSHOP

Go back to Route 325 and turn left, then left again after 100m/yds. Almost immediately on the right is **Ban Pinsuwan Benjarong** ❺ (32/1 Moo 7, Bangchang; daily 8am–noon, 1–5pm, workshop closed Sun pm). The owner of this small family workshop, Virat Pinsuwan, is an antiques restorer who was inspired to make Benjarong pieces (see page 20) using traditional designs. He has become so successful that orders take eight months to fill. Take a tour, watch craftsmen work, and consider buying from a small selection of items. There is also a small ceramics museum.

DON HOI LOT

Go back to Route 325, turn left and do a U-turn after 100m/yds. This road runs all the way to the town of Samut Songkhram, from where the nearby Don Hoi Lot is an ideal place to lunch before heading back to Bangkok.

At the end of Route 325 turn right and follow the main road through town until it brings you onto Rama II Road. Go over the bridge, which follows a loop onto Highway 35. After 2km (1.25 miles) leave the highway following signs to Don Hoi Lot, then do a U-turn after 100m/yds.

About 6km (4 miles) further on is **Don Hoi Lot** ❻, where seafood stalls line the road and restaurants jut out on wooden piers into the Mae Khlong River Delta. Stop at **Khun Pao Restaurant**, see ❷, where you can try the *hoi lot* (razor clams) that give the area its name. If you are lucky and the water is low, you will see the fossilised remains of the clams sticking out of the mud close to shore.

To return to Bangkok, go back to Highway 35 and do a U-turn according to the signs. The drive is about one hour.

Food and drink

❶ CHEDI SQUARE FOOD STALLS

Thanon Khwa Phra; $

There is a variety of food stalls opposite the *chedi* where, along with regular Thai dishes, you will find local specialities such as pink pomelos and *khao lam* (black beans, palm sugar and sticky rice grilled in tubes of hollow bamboo).

❷ KHUN PAO RESTAURANT

1/3 Moo 4, Don Hoi Lot; tel: 0 3472 3703; $

A rustic spot overlooking the Mae Khlong River Delta. The speciality is seafood, including the celebrated *hoi lot* (razor clams), unappetisingly referred to as 'worm shells' on the menu. Delicious nevertheless.

KANCHANABURI

Drive west to visit a laid-back town with a dark history: it was here that the Bridge on the River Kwai and 'Death Railway' were built during World War II. Afterwards, lighten the mood with an exhilarating trek and a swim in a waterfall.

DISTANCE: Bangkok to Kanchanaburi: 130km (75 miles); Kanchanaburi tour: 7.25km (4.5 miles)

TIME: One or two days

START: Bridge on the River Kwai

END: Kanchanaburi War Cemetery

POINTS TO NOTE: It is best to hire a car to get to Kanchanaburi. Leave Bangkok west on Highway 4, head 10km (6 miles) past Nakhon Pathom, then follow Route 323 to Kanchanaburi. If you go by train or bus, you can get around town by tuk tuk or *songthaew* (open-backed taxi vans) for around B30 a go, or hire motorbikes and bicycles along River Kwai Road. The route can be done as a busy day trip; alternatively, stay overnight and explore Erawan National Park on day two. For overnight options, see page 83.

BRIDGE ON THE RIVER KWAI

Kanchanaburi is well worth the two- to three-hour drive it takes to get there. The town is famous as the location of the **Bridge on the River Kwai** ❶, part of the 'Death Railway' built by prisoners of the occupying Japanese forces in World War II. The story of how some 16,000 Allied POWs and up to 100,000 Asian slave labourers died during the construction was told in the 1957 film *Bridge on the River Kwai*, directed by David Lean and starring Alec Guinness. Parts of the bridge are original, but the central arches were rebuilt following Allied bombing in the war. Period steam trains are parked close by, with more at the main railway station on Saeng Chuto Road.

You can walk across the bridge, but gaps in the planking reveal long drops into the river, so people have to shuffle carefully around each other on the firm central plates between the tracks. Niches between the spans provide a refuge in case a rare train happens along.

The railway was built to link what was then Burma to Japanese positions in the rest of Asia, both as a supply route and to exploit the country's natural resources. It is said that one prisoner died for every sleeper laid.

Bridge on the River Kwai

WORLD WAR II MUSEUM

From the bridge walk 50m/yds along River Kwai Road, past the shops, to reach the **World War II Museum** ❷ (395–403 River Kwai Road; daily 8am–5pm) on the right. Despite its name, this eccentric collection is in many ways a vanity project for the family that owns it; one of the two buildings here has a celebration of the family achievements on the top floor. The rest includes artefacts from Thai history and an art collection as well as war-related items. There are the remains of a wooden footbridge built by prisoners to cross the river, plus weapons and vehicles. Despite a slightly tacky ambience and poorly labelled exhibits, this is still an entertaining diversion. On the road next to the museum is a Japanese War Memorial Shrine.

LUNCH STOP

Leaving the museum, drive away from the bridge along River Kwai Road, which bends left after 1.5km (1 mile). Then bear right where the road forks and drive for another 150m/yds, where the road narrows between rows of low shops. At the small crossroads turn right. At the lights bear left (not over the bridge), then continue straight ahead again at the next lights, where you will come to a long stretch of river front lined with floating restaurants and cafés. Although much of the food is only so-so,

this is an atmospheric place to stop off for lunch; try **Tara Buree**, see ❶. You will find boats for hire too, if you want a river trip. Continue past the restaurants up the hill to the end and turn right into Chaichumpol Road.

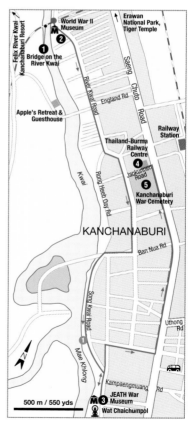

JEATH War Museum

JEATH WAR MUSEUM

After another 500m/yds you will come to a temple called Wat Chaichumpol. Adjacent to it is the **JEATH War Museum** ❸ (daily 8am–6pm), founded in 1977 by a monk called Phra Theppanyasuthee, who later became abbot of the temple. The museum is named after the countries whose dead it is intended to commemorate: Japan, England, America, Australia, Thailand and Holland. The building – which is modelled on one of the bamboo huts in which prisoners of war were incarcerated – contains newspaper clippings, personal items such as photographs and clothes, and drawings by ex-prisoners depicting their life in the camps.

RAILWAY CENTRE

Head back along Thanon Chaichumpol, and then turn right through the monumental white city gates. Beyond the city pillar, take a left at the traffic lights along

the Saeng Chuto Road, then left again after 2km (1.25 miles) into Jaokunnen Road, where the **Thailand–Burma Railway Centre** ❹ (www.tbrconline.com; daily 9am–5pm), the latest of Kanchanaburi's war-related museums, is situated 50m/yds on the right at No. 73.

The two-floor exhibition space starts with a timeline and useful maps plotting Japanese expansion in Asia and then moves through videos, models and photos showing the prisoners' living and working conditions. During a push to complete the railway quickly, increased labour hours and poor nutrition caused the deaths of 7,000 prisoners in a five-month period to October 1943. A model of a hospital hut, with dioramas of amputations being performed, details the medical staff's struggles to cope with equipment improvised from found objects such as old bicycles.

On the second floor exhibits include moving personal items such as diary entries and letters from home. A café on site has snack meals and drinks.

WAR CEMETERY

Opposite the museum is the **Kanchanaburi War Cemetery** ❺, where the 7,000 Australian, British and Dutch casualties of the Death Railway are buried or commemorated (the US dead have been repatriated). Despite the tourist buses, the cemetery retains its serenity and is very moving. There is a museum tracing how the men lived their final days.

War Cemetery

BLUE SAPPHIRES

Kanchanaburi is also well known for blue sapphires, which are mined north of town in Bo Phloi. You can buy them in the small shopping plaza near the River Kwai Bridge, but as this is a tourist area, prices are inflated and you will need to bargain hard for a good deal. To avoid scams, it is best to find shops with licences displayed on the wall and avoid the street touts.

OPTIONAL SECOND DAY

From here you can either head back to Bangkok or stay to explore other attractions in this largely unspoilt region. Overnight options include **Apple's Retreat & Guesthouse** (see page 106) or any of the budget accommodation found along the River Kwai Road, or the **Felix River Kwai Kanchanaburi Resort**, which has good river-view rooms (see page 106). **The Keereetara Restaurant** (see page 117), close to the bridge, is a lovely spot for dinner.

Erawan National Park

Depending on how much you want to see, day two could be long, so start as early as you can. Leave Kanchanaburi, heading northwest for 65km (40 miles) along Route 3199 until you come to the main entrance of **Erawan National Park** (www.dnp.go.th; daily 8am–4.30pm). There are also buses from Kanchanaburi that drop you at Erawan Village. From there, take a

songthaew to the park entrance 2km (1.25 miles) away.

The park's main attraction is the seven-tiered **Erawan Waterfall**, named after the three-headed elephant from Hindu mythology. The best time to visit is during – or just after – the rainy season (May–Nov), when the water is at full flow. There are lots of stopping points if you can't make it all the way to the top (a two-hour trek). Remember to take food and water with you.

There are several hiking trails in the park, which comprises mainly deciduous forests with limestone hills. One of the most popular hiking options is the 90-minute Khanmak-Mookling trail; the 1,400-metre (0.85-mile) circular route starts from the national park office. Also taking approximately 90 minutes, the Wangbadan Cave trail takes you through bamboo and evergreen forests along a 1,350-metre route.

From Erawan retrace the route to Bangkok.

Food and drink

1 TARA BUREE

48 Song Kwai Road; tel: 0 3451 2944; $

This floating restaurant juts into the river on several pontoons. The view compensates for the basic dishes such as deep-fried prawns with garlic and steamed sea bass with lemon sauce.

Erawan Museum

SAMUT PRAKAN

Just south of Bangkok are two extraordinary museum projects that preserve Thai heritage: one housed inside an extraordinary, giant, three-headed elephant, the other a replica of the whole country, replete with life-size temples and palaces.

DISTANCE: Bangkok to Erawan Museum: 20km (12 miles)
TIME: A full day
START: Erawan Museum
END: The Ancient City
POINTS TO NOTE: Take Thanon Sukhumvit to Soi 117, then follow signs to Thanon Kanchanapisek. Turn left towards Bangna and U-turn under the bridge. The Erawan Museum is on the left. For the Ancient City, head left (south) on Thanon Sukhumvit. At Pak Nam turn left. The Ancient City is on the left at Km 33. Alternatively, bus 511 (air-conditioned) goes from Ekamai Bus Station, stopping at Erawan Museum and Pak Nam, where you change to minibus No. 36 to the Ancient City.

The road southeast from Bangkok runs close to the Chao Phraya River and the urban sprawl continues with fish factories and packing plants. But the province of Samut Prakan (part of the Bangkok metropolis) has two extraordinary sites.

ERAWAN MUSEUM

The **Erawan Museum** ❶ (Sukhumvit Soi 119; www.muangboranmuseum.com; daily 9am–7pm) is housed in a 43m (141ft) -high three-headed elephant that represents Erawan, the animal ridden by the god Indra in Hindu mythology. It was created by philanthropist Lek Viriyaphant, whose other projects include the Ancient City (see below) and the Sanctuary of Truth, in Pattaya (see page 96).

The museum is in three sections: 'Underworld' (Chinese and Thai antiques); 'Earth' (work by the country's most celebrated craftsmen); and 'Heaven' (abstract murals and antique Buddha statues, showcased in the elephant's hollow belly).

THE ANCIENT CITY

From the museum, turn left on Thanon Sukhumvit and drive for 11.5km (7 miles) to the **Ancient City** ❷ (Muang Boran; www.muangboranmuseum.com; daily 9am–7pm) on the left. The

Statue at the Ancient City   *Pavilion in the Ancient City*

parkland site is loosely shaped to represent Thailand, with over 100 monuments, palaces and other buildings placed approximately in their correct geographical location. Some are life-size or nearly life-size reproductions of long-lost structures; others are buildings that were relocated here.

It could take four hours to tour the site, either in your car, bicycle, golf cart or guided tram tour, all available at the gate. For highlights, head to the Central region, where the centrepiece is a reconstruction

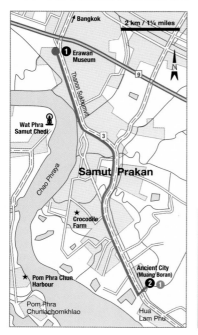

of the 15th-century Sanphet Prasat Palace, the main royal residence of the early Ayutthaya period. It was notable because it heralded a new architecture that differed from the earlier Khmer and Sukhothai styles in details such as tapering pillars, pedimented door frames and overlapping roofing. This Ayutthaya School dominated the landscape well into the Rattanakosin era four centuries later. The palace was completely destroyed when the Burmese sacked Ayutthaya in 1767.

Close by are other replica monuments of the country's rich 'Rice Bowl', such as the beautiful Dusit Maha Prasat Palace and the Phra Kaew Pavilion from the current Grand Palace in Bangkok. The site also has period houses of various styles and mock-ups of regional villages with local crafts for sale.

There are open-air cafés in the grounds, notably near the **Floating Market**, see ❶.

For a break from hard heritage, the nearby Samut Prakan Crocodile Farm (555 Moo 7, Tai Baan, Samut Prakan; daily 8am–6pm) is reputed to be the biggest in the world.

Food and drink

❶ FLOATING MARKET

The Ancient City; $

The small cafés here include Rim Naam. Spicy Thai salads and one-plate dishes such as garlic chicken on rice are typical.

Wehat Chanrun Palace

AYUTTHAYA

Take a trip into Thailand's glorious past, when its ancient capital Ayutthaya had 2,000 golden temples, a population of a million, and trade links that stretched from Holland to China.

DISTANCE: 76km (48 miles) from Bangkok to Ayutthaya
TIME: A full day
START: Bang Pa-In
END: Ayutthaya
POINTS TO NOTE: There are regular buses and trains, but it is best reached by car (one hour). From Bangkok take either northbound express route, then follow signs to Bang Pa-In. To see all the sites travel Wed–Sun.

Ayutthaya is built on an island surrounded by the Chao Phraya, Pa Sak and Lop Buri rivers. It was the wealthy capital of Thailand (then known as Siam) until it was destroyed in 1767 by invading Burmese armies, who looted and burnt everything in their path. Their city in ruins, the inhabitants fled.

Today those ruins form the Ayutthaya Historical Park, a Unesco World Heritage Site that is tantalisingly suggestive of a cosmopolitan metropolis, with quarters occupied by Chinese, Portuguese, French and countless other nationalities. A pleasant detour en route from Bangkok is the royal retreat of Bang Pa-In.

BANG PA-IN

The lovely palace complex of **Bang Pa-In ❶** (daily 8am–3.30pm), located 20km (12.5 miles) south of Ayutthaya, is arranged around a man-made lake, with many structures on small islands accessed by walkways and bridges. Thailand's rulers came here as long ago as the 17th century, but the current collection of buildings dates from the reigns of kings Rama IV (1851–68) and Rama V (1868–1910). The mix of Thai, Chinese, Gothic and neo-classical architecture is typical of the latter's reign.

There are buggies available at the main entrance (charge), if you would prefer not to walk around the complex.

Shrines and pavilions

From the entrance you pass **Ho Hem**

Exploring Ayutthaya's ruins

Phra Thinang Aisawan Tippaya-Art pavilion

Monthian Thewarat, a Khmer-style shrine dedicated to King Prasat Thong of Ayutthaya, who built the original palace here. Ahead to the left in the middle of the lake is **Phra Thinang Aisawan Tippaya-Art** (Divine Seat of Personal Freedom), a magnificent Thai-style pavilion with a spired roof. It is a copy of the Arporn Phimok Prasat in the Grand Palace in Bangkok (see page 31), and contains a bronze statue of King Rama V in military uniform.

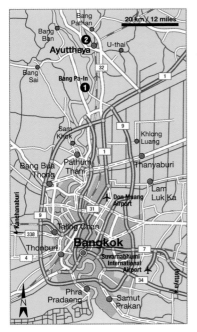

Garden of Secured Land

An island hop away is the **Phra Thinang Uthayan Phumisathian** (Garden of Secured Land), where King Rama V preferred to stay. The original two-storey wooden structure, built in 1877, was destroyed by fire in 1938, and this reconstruction was completed in 1996 during the current king's Golden Jubilee year. Only the Gothic water tower remains of the original building.

Other notable features include the classical Chinese **Wehat Chanrun Palace** and, on the other side of the river from the palace and reached by cable car, **Wat Nivet Dhammaparvat**, which with all its Gothic styling and stained-glass windows could be mistaken for a Christian church.

AYUTTHAYA

Leaving Bang Pa-In, turn left from the gate and take the road around the back of the palace along a lane where traditional houses on stilts line the Chao Phraya River. At the junction turn left and follow signs to **Ayutthaya ❷**. At the end of this road turn right towards Route 32, where you turn left and drive after a few kilometres over the Naresuan Bridge into Ayutthaya. The journey from Bang Pa-In takes approximately 20 minutes.

Ayutthaya Historical Study Centre

Continue along Thanon Rotchana and

Colourful glass windows

turn left into the **Ayutthaya Historical Study Centre** Ⓐ (Thanon Rotchana; daily 9am–4pm), which is divided into five sections covering the ancient city as capital, state and port, plus traditions and village life. It gives a good introductory overview of this once powerful city.

Founded by King Uthong in 1350, Ayutthaya soon took the kingdom of Sukhothai under its rule; the city's influence eventually spread as far as Angkor to the east and Pegu (in what was then Burma) to the west. By the early 1500s the Portuguese, and later the Dutch, British and French, were regular visitors, and Ayutthayan kings engaged Japanese soldiers, Indian

men-at-arms and Persian ministers to serve in their retinues.

As the Burmese armies triumphed in 1767, not only were the city's monuments destroyed, but also most official records, in effect ripping the cultural heart from the nation. It was for this reason that King Rama I was committed to creating Bangkok in Ayutthaya's image when he chose it for his new capital in 1782.

Turning left from the centre, near the junction on the right is the **Chao Sam Phraya Museum** Ⓑ (Thanon Rotchana; daily 9am–4pm), which houses relics discovered around the city, including Buddha images, carvings, stucco work and period art.

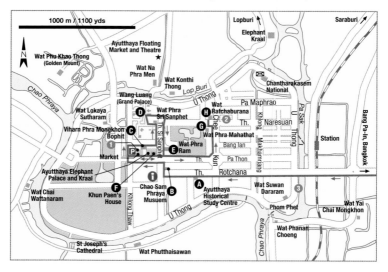

Wat Mahathat   *Buddha head in tree roots, Wat Phra Mahathat*

Viharn Phra Mongkhon Bophit

Turn right at the top of the road into Thanon Si Sanphet and go left at the roundabout into Thanon Pha Thon. Turn right just before the bridge over the canal, and after a short way turn into the car park on your right.

The car park leads immediately to a **market** (daily 7am–6pm), which sells crafts, souvenirs and food, and also has **food stalls**, see ❶, in the central area, if you're ready for refreshment.

The large red temple roof to the rear of the market identifies **Viharn Phra Mongkhon Bophit** ❻ (daily 8am–4.30pm). Although itself a new building, the temple is venerated for its massive 15th-century bronze Buddha, which had lain unsheltered amid the ruins here for two centuries until the *viharn* (sermon hall) was built to house it in 1956. There are black-and-white photos on the walls showing the statue in its previous condition. While the rest of old Ayutthaya sites are thronged by foreign tourists, this one is a hotspot for Thai worshippers, particularly at weekends.

Wat Phra Sri Sanphet

Take the path on the left of the entrance to the walled **Wat Phra Sri Sanphet** (daily 8am–6pm). This royal temple was built in 1491 to honour three 15th-century kings, whose remains are housed in the trio of restored *chedis* standing in a line. These structures have appeared on hundreds of postcards and magazine pages, and are perhaps the most photographed images of Ayutthaya. The Burmese melted the gold off the 16m (52ft) -high main standing Buddha image here, and the remains were later removed by King Rama I (and concealed inside Chedi Sri Sanphet at Bangkok's Wat Pho).

Ruined stupas and *chedis* littering the grounds give a glimpse of what the city must have been like when visiting European dignitaries wrote awed accounts of great wealth and 2,000 temple spires clad in gold. At the time its 1 million population was greater than that of London.

Grand Palace

Beyond the wall opposite the wat's entrance is the location of the **Grand Palace** ❼ (Wang Luang), although only the brick foundations remain (an impressive reproduction of the palace can be seen at the Ancient City, see page 84). King Borom Trai Lokanath built the royal residence here in 1448 after abandoning King Uthong's original wooden palace (on the site later occupied by Wat Phra Sri Sanphet). The Grand Palace was razed by the Burmese, and the bricks removed to Bangkok to build the city's defensive walls.

Wat Phra Ram

Facing the palace from Wat Phra Sri Sanphet, turn right along the side of

Khun Paen's House

the temple wall and right at the end, past the statue of King Uthong. Ahead to the left is **Wat Phra Ram ⓔ** (daily 8am–6pm), which, having been constructed in 1369 by Uthong's son King Ramesuan, is one of the city's oldest temples. It was built on the site of his father's cremation, and has been restored twice. Elephant gates punctuate the old walls, and the central terrace is dominated by a crumbling *prang* (Khmer-style tower) with a gallery of stucco Naga serpents, garudas and Buddha statues.

Khun Paen's House

Come out of Wat Phra Ram into the park opposite. Walk 100m/yds along the right side of the lake and cross over it via the first wooden bridge. On the other side is **Khun Paen's**

Shopping in Wat Phra Mahathat

House ⓕ, which, although empty of furnishings, is a good example of a traditional Thai abode, showing the three separate dwellings of the extended family arranged around a communal veranda for socialising and eating. People habitually ate sitting on the floor, which is the original reason for taking your shoes off when entering a Thai building. It was rebuilt here in 1940, the location of the original city jail. From the house, the view appears to be an idyllic country scene. Many traditional houses in Bangkok, including part of Jim Thompson's home (see page 61), were relocated from Ayutthaya.

Wat Phra Mahathat

Now it's time to reclaim your car if you have one. Turn left from the car park and take the first left back into Thanon Pha Thon. At the second roundabout, turn left into Thanon Maharat, then left again into the car park at **Wat Phra Mahathat ⓖ** (daily 8am–6pm). Souvenir shops here mark this out as being one of the most visited (and most atmospheric) temples.

The complex originally dates from the late 14th century and the reign of King Ramesuan, although it was largely restored around 1663 by King Prasat Thong. Wat Mahathat was one of the most important temples in Ayutthaya's heyday: the seat of the Supreme Patriarch and with a *prang* that stood around 50m (164ft) high.

Remains of a Buddha image at Wat Ratchaburana

From the entrance gate, walk to the right to find a stone Buddha head on the ground trapped in the tangled roots of a bodhi tree. It is one of the iconic images of Ayutthaya. Around the ruins are numerous headless statues, with just the crossed legs hinting at the meditative positions they once assumed. The Wat Mahathat grounds are large enough to enable you to enjoy serene moments even when accompanied by coach parties.

Wat Ratchaburana

Turn left out of Wat Mahathat and cross the road, where, on the corner, there is another of the city's most significant sites. King Borom Ratchathirat II (Chao Sam Phraya) built **Wat Ratchaburana** ⊕ (Thanon Maharat; daily 8am–6pm) in 1424 as a memorial to his elder brothers who killed each other at this spot in an elephant-back duel for the throne. Some murals still exist, while other artworks found during excavations in the late 1950s are now kept in the Chao Sam Phraya Museum.

Across Thanon Maharat on the corner of Thanon Naresuan is **Ruean Rojjana**, see ②, if you are hungry at this point.

BACK TO BANGKOK

To leave Ayutthaya, do a U-turn from Wat Ratchaburana and turn left by Ruean Rojjana into Thanon Naresuan.

Drive to the end of the road and turn right, then right again just before the bridge. If you go straight ahead, you will come to **Pae Krung Kao Ayudthaya**, see ③, an alternative meal stop 200m/yds on the left. Follow the road round to go over the bridge and on to Bangkok.

Food and drink

① FOOD STALLS

Central Market, Viharn Phra Mongkhon Bophit; daily 9am–6pm; $

Diners sit at communal tables ringed by individual vendors selling dishes like Thai omelettes, curries and noodle soups with pork and chicken.

② RUEAN ROJJANA

22/13 Thanon Maharat; tel: 0 3532 3765; www.rueanrojjana.com; daily 10am–8.30pm; $$

With outside tables and traditional triangular cushion seating with wat views, this spot serves tourist favourites such as *tom yum goong* and fried chicken with cashew nuts.

③ PAE KRUNG KAO AYUDTHAYA

Km 4, Moo 2, Thanon Authong; tel: 0 3524 1555; daily 10am–9pm; $

This large but cosy restaurant on the riverbank is a picturesque spot to enjoy curries and spicy salads, or a whole fried fish eaten with dipping sauces.

Wat Yai Suwannaram

PHETCHABURI

Feast on some of Thailand's best-loved desserts while picking up the flavour of old-fashioned Siam in a small town of 18th-century Ayutthaya-period temples, and the summer palace of King Rama IV.

DISTANCE: 132km (84 miles) from Bangkok to Phetchaburi; town tour: 5.5km (3.5 miles)
TIME: A full day
START: Wat Yai Suwannaram
END: Phra Nakhon Khiri Park
POINTS TO NOTE: By public transport, the journey takes about 3 hours; the drive takes about 90 mins. Buses run from Bangkok's Southern Bus Terminal; trains from Hualamphong Station. By car, take Highway 35 west, then Highway 4 south; on the way back, look out for the road branching left to Samut Songkram to get back onto Highway 35 (there is no sign for Bangkok).

Phetchaburi – usually pronounced Petburi – was once a significant port, from where goods were ferried by river and canal to the old Siam capital of Ayutthaya. King Rama IV was one of several kings of the current Chakri dynasty who chose this coastal area as a place to escape the seasonal Bangkok heat.

LOCAL TEMPLES

The town's wats are open daily 8am–4pm. Start at **Wat Yai Suwannaram** ❶ on Phongsuriya Road, thought to have once been a residence of King Suea. Its fine murals are among the country's oldest.

Turn right out of the wat, then right onto Phokarong Road, where **Wat Kamphaeng Laeng** ❷ is 800m/yds up on the right. The sandstone wall of the compound is partly original, as are four Khmer-style *prangs*, one of which contains a Buddha footprint relic.

Next, turn right down Phra Song Road for about 1km (0.6 miles). At the crossroads with Matayawong Road, turn left. After 800m/yds turn right at the clock tower to find **Wat Ko Keo Sutharam** ❸, 50m/yds on the left. The murals here, which date from 1734, depict the previous lives of the Buddha.

On leaving, turn left on to Phanit Charoen Road. After 800m/yds turn left at Phra Song Road and follow it to the white tower of **Wat Mahathat** ❹, which contains murals and a statue of five Buddhas.

Traditional sweets   _View over Khao Wang_

DAY MARKET

Retrace your steps on Phra Song Road and turn left into Phanit Charoen Road, where the **Day Market** ❺ is 150m/yds on the right. It's a good place to sample the local desserts, including _khao chae_, rice in jasmine-infused water, served with stuffed chillis or fresh fruit.

KING'S RETREAT

Stay on Phanit Charoen Road then turn left after 100m/yds onto Chisa-In Road, which soon crosses the river. Take the next right, then left at Ratchawithi Road, and continue 1.5km (1 mile) to the end, passing the **Krua Thai** café, see ❶. Directly ahead you can start the ascent to **Phra Nakhon Khiri Historical Park** ❻ (www.phranakhonkhiri. com; daily 8.30am–4pm). If you don't want to climb, turn right, then left at the traffic lights. After the green overhead signs to Bangkok, go left at the road marked 'cable car'. After 200m/yds a white building marks another entrance to the park and funicular rail access (charge). There are places for snacks here, too. Don't take food with you: the hillside is populated by potentially aggressive monkeys.

Amid the trees at the top are several temples and a **summer palace** of King Rama IV (1851–68), who was the subject of several books and the film _The King & I_, based on the memoirs of Anna Leonowens. The building is very modest, and the king's own quarters positively cell-like, perhaps befitting someone who spent many years in a monastery before ascending the throne.

Food and drink

❶ KRUA THAI

Thai 57 Ratchawithi Road; tel: 0 3242 6941; $
Air-conditioned café serving rice dishes, fish, stir-fries and soups.

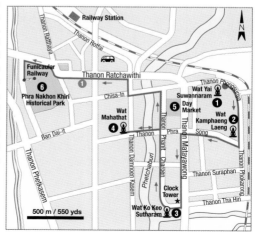

Hua Hin railway station

HUA HIN

Despite its modern role as a tourist attraction, this small seaside town retains an air of tranquillity and has been favoured as a summer seat by the royal family since the early 20th century.

DISTANCE: 195km (121 miles) Bangkok to Hua Hin; town tour: 15.5km (9.6 miles)
TIME: A full day
START: Hua Hin Railway Station
END: Hua Hin Night Market
POINTS TO NOTE: If driving, take Highway 35 then Highway 4 (2.5–3 hours). Buses run from Bangkok's Southern Bus Terminal. Trains go from Hualamphong Station. Both take three to four hours. The last bus to Bangkok leaves at 9pm, and the last train is 4pm, so staying the night is the best option. For hotels, see page 107. Without Khao Takiab, this tour is walkable.

Prachuap Kiri Khan is Thailand's narrowest province and its coast is fringed with mountains and lovely quiet beaches, the most popular of which is a long sandy one at Hua Hin.

The town gained royal favour when King Rama VI built a seafront summer palace here in 1922. **Phra Ratchawang Klai Kangwon** (Far From Worries Palace) led to an influx of high society, and so began the sleepy fishing village's transformation into a tourist hotspot.

RAILWAY STATION

Built in 1923, **Hua Hin Railway Station** ① is the town's second-most famous building, and the dainty teak structure has much of its original charm. Across the single-rail track (one of Thailand's first rail lines) is the **Royal Hua Hin Golf Course** (Damnern Kasem Road; www.golfhuahin. com; daily 6am–6pm), built in 1924.

Leave the station, go down Damnern Kasem Road and turn right at the traffic lights into Phetchakasem Road. After 3km (2 miles) bear left beside the flyover, following signs to Khao Takiab. On the left, beside signs to the Hyatt Regency Hua Hin (see page 108), is the site of the weekend Cicada Market.

KHAO TAKIAB

After 2.5km (1.5 miles) go left at the major fork, follow the road as it bends left and head uphill to the summit of **Khao**

| Royal golf course | Hua Hin's coastline |

Takiab ② (Chopstick Hill). Here there are souvenir stalls, cafés and a temple where a tree shades Buddha images and monkeys feed on bananas from tourists. A narrow road circling the summit has views of the Gulf of Thailand, as does **La Mer** restaurant (tel: 0 3253 6205), which serves Thai food.

COLONIAL HOTELS

Driving back to town, turn right at the traffic lights into Damnern Kasem Road. At the bottom of the slope go right and then left into the **Centara Grand Beach Resort & Villas ③**, Thailand's first resort accommodation when it was built as the Railway Hotel in 1923. The beautifully preserved colonial setting ensures it is a popular film location, including in *The Killing Fields* (1984). Have afternoon tea in **The Museum**, a pavilion benefitting from gentle breezes and views of the gardens and sea.

SHOPPING

Afterwards, wander onto the beach and turn left. After 50m/yds go left beside the pony hire, continue for 100m/yds and turn right into **Naresdamri Road ④**, with Thai massage, Indian tailors, bars and restaurants.

After 200m/yds you come to **Chaolay Seafood**, see ①, and beyond that **Brasserie de Paris** (see page 117). Opposite Chao Lay is Hua Hin Soi 57; turn left here and cross two main roads (Naeb Khaehat

and Phetchakasem) into Decha Nuchit Road, where **Hua Hin Night Market ⑤** (daily 5–11pm) is a great place to sample street food and stock up on Thai silks.

Food and drink

① CHAOLAY SEAFOOD
15 Naresdamri Road; tel: 0 3251 3436; $$
This fish restaurant is one of the best of several eateries on stilts over the sea.

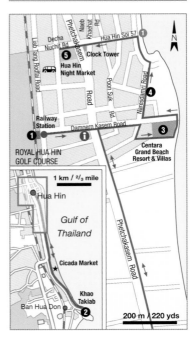

Sanctuary of Truth

PATTAYA

After a relaxing afternoon amid tropical gardens and a carved wooden temple overlooking the waves, change pace and head for Pattaya's pulsating nightlife, full of bars and bands and the sequinned excess of ladyboy cabaret.

DISTANCE: 140km (87 miles) to Pattaya; town tour via Nong Nooch: 55km (33.5 miles)
TIME: A full day
START: The Sanctuary of Truth
END: Beach Road
POINTS TO NOTE: By car (2-hour drive) from Bangkok, take Highway 7 east then south; it joins Sukhumvit Road at Pattaya. Buses go every 30 minutes, 5am–10pm, from Bangkok's Eastern Bus Terminal. Hail a *songthaew* (pick-up truck) to tour Pattaya.

Pattaya may be notorious for its sex trade – a legacy of US soldiers on leave during the Vietnam War – but less raunchy attractions also entice families.

With a 10am start from Bangkok you will arrive in time for a seafront lunch. Entering Pattaya from Highway 7, turn right, then after 500m/yds go left into Naklua Road. After 300m/yds turn right into Naklua Soi 4, where you can lunch at **Mumaroi**, see ❶, on the left.

THE SANCTUARY OF TRUTH

Turn right from the restaurant and rejoin Naklua Road, driving straight ahead into the old fishing village of Naklua. Look out for the spirit tree where fishermen leave offerings in the hope of safety and a good catch. After 3km (2 miles) turn right into Naklua Soi 12. Bearing left where the road forks, you will come to the first sight on this tour, the **Sanctuary of Truth** ❶ (www.sanctuaryoftruth.com; daily 8am–6pm), which appears like a fairy-tale castle on

Food and drink

❶ MUMAROI
83/4 Moo 2, Naklua Soi 4; tel: 0 3822 3252; $$
Fabulous seafood accompanied by a sea view from the open-air terrace.

❷ KING SEAFOOD
94 Walking Street; tel: 0 3842 9459; $$
Try super-fresh fish at this eatery on stilts overlooking the sea.

Ladyboy performer

the water's edge. Over 100m (328ft) high and a work in progress, it is made entirely of hardwoods, intricately carved with figures of gods and spirits.

NONG NOOCH

Leave the sanctuary, turn right at Nak-lua Road, and follow the road until you reach a roundabout. You could bear right to reach Beach Road. Alternatively, to visit an adventure park, turn left into North Pattaya Road and right at the top into Sukhumvit Road. After 22.5km (14 miles) turn left to **Nong Nooch ②** (163 Sukhumvit Road, Sattaheep; www.nongnooch tropicalgarden.com; daily 9am–6pm), famed for its botanical gardens, elephants and zoo.

TIFFANY'S CABARET

From Nong Nooch, return on the route to Pattaya, turning left at Central Pattaya Road, then right at the crossroads into Pattaya 2nd Road. After 1km (0.6 miles), on the left beside Soi Srinakorn is **Tiffany's ③** (464 Moo 9, Pattaya 2nd Road; tel: 0 3842 1700; www.tiffany-show. co.th; shows at 6pm, 7.30pm and 9pm), which hosts Thailand's famous ladyboy (katoey) shows.

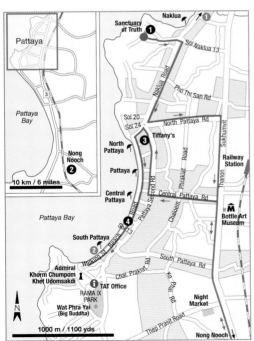

BEACH ROAD

Turn left from Tiffany's, then left again at the roundabout into **Beach Road ④**. Park somewhere around Soi 13. The roads are awash with market stalls, shopping malls and go-go bars. The extension of Beach Road is **Walking Street**, where you will find **King Seafood**, see ②.

DIRECTORY

Hand-picked hotels and restaurants to suit all budgets and tastes, organised by area, plus select nightlife listings, an alphabetical listing of practical information, a language guide and an overview of the best books and films to give you a flavour of the city.

Millennium Hilton Bangkok

ACCOMMODATION

Thailand is no longer the ultra-cheap destination of backpacker folklore but Bangkok still has very affordable accommodation, particularly around the Khao San Road area. Many moderately priced hotels in Bangkok have excellent facilities, and even budget hotels often have a swimming pool and at least one decent food outlet. Those on a tight budget will find numerous guesthouses with clean accommodation plus air-conditioning and en suite bathrooms.

Further up the chain, development has been rapid, which means prices remain competitive from mid-range to luxury and there's an increasing spread of boutique properties around the city.

Advance hotel bookings are advised for the holiday periods at Christmas, New Year and Chinese New Year (Feb or Mar), and for the Songkran festival in mid-April.

Many mid-price and top-end hotels charge a standard 7 percent VAT and 10 percent service charge, so check to see if the quoted rate includes them. Depending on the season, discounts can exceed 50 percent or more off the published rack rate. It pays to shop around. As rates can

be so elastic, relative price categories denoting the lowest priced rooms available are used in this section; this is a guide price only. Internet prices are often lower; visit hotel websites or online hotel sites such as www.agoda.com.

Rattanakosin

Arun Residence & Sala Arun

38 Soi Pratoo Nok Yoong; tel: 0 2221 9158; www.arunresidence.com; $$

Situated in an old Sino-Portuguese mansion on a residential street, this tiny boutique hotel is just a short walk from Wat Pho. One side of it perches on the bank of the Chao Phraya River, offering views of Wat Arun. Its Euro-Thai restaurant, The Deck, is an atmospheric spot. They have a beautiful sister residence, Sala Arun (www.salaarun.com), just down the river.

Chakrabongse Villas

396 Thanon Maharat; tel: 0 2222 1290; www.chakrabongsevillas.com; $$$$

This compound was built in 1908 as the home of a Thai prince (some of his family still live here). Four Thai-style villas sit in an elegant setting overlooking the river and Wat Arun. Beautiful gardens and a secluded pool add to its appeal, as does close proximity to the Grand Palace, a 15-minute walk away.

Thonburi

Anantara Bangkok Riverside Resort

Price for a double room without breakfast and taxes:
$$$$ = more than B8,000
$$$ = B4,000–8,000
$$ = B2,000–4,000
$ = less than B2,000

& Spa

257 Thanon Charoen Nakhon; tel: 0 2476 0022; www.bangkok-riverside.anantara.com; $$$

It is a peaceful 15-minute boat ride to this resort with lush grounds and a river-front pool, making it a relaxing escape from the city. There are regular shuttle boats downtown, but if you would rather not go anywhere, there are six restaurants, three bars and the divine Mandara Spa onsite. The Riverside Terrace hosts Thai dance-drama over dinner.

Millennium Hilton Bangkok

123 Thanon Charoen Nakhon; tel: 0 2442 2000; www3.hilton.com; $$$

The swish Hilton has a stylish modern Asian interior designed by Tony Chi. All rooms have expansive windows with river views and the pool has a resort feel. There is a spa, four restaurants and two bars, plus a complimentary shuttle boat service to the Bangkok side.

The Peninsula Bangkok

333 Thanon Charoen Nakhon; tel: 0 2861 2888; www.peninsula.com; $$$$

The contemporary international decor has neat Asian undertones, and all rooms overlook the Chao Phraya, although a new condominium, The River, now partially restricts views to the south. There's a lovely spa, a pool overlooking the river, and the superb Chinese restaurant Mei Jeang is one of the best in the city. A free shuttle boat is available to Saphan Taksin BTS station from 6am–midnight.

Old City and Dusit

Buddy Lodge

265 Thanon Khao San; tel: 0 2629 4477; www.buddylodge.com; $

Khao San's pioneering boutique hotel at the beginning of the century, Buddy Lodge has a rooftop swimming pool, fitness room and a well-run spa. The rooms are more cute than plush, but are en suite with wood walls, louvred windows, small balconies and satellite TV. Located in a mini mall with bars, shops and a McDonald's downstairs.

D&D Inn

68–70 Thanon Khao San; tel: 0 2629 0526–8; www.khaosanby.com; $

Right in the middle of Khao San, this is more of a hotel than guesthouse, with a rooftop swimming pool, bar and an open pavilion for traditional massage. The 200 rooms are well equipped with bathroom, air-conditioning, TV, fridge and IDD phone.

Old Capital Bike Inn

609 Thanon Phra Sumen; tel: 0 2629 1787; www.oldcapitalbkk.com; $$

With teak furniture and fittings this 10-room hotel is a gem of traditional Thai character, set in a late 19th-century royal home. The rooms and suites each have a floral theme, and some have split level accommodation. Installed in each room are satellite TVs, DVD players, broadband internet, and even computers. It is close to the Golden Mount and well situated for the Old City attractions.

Dream Hotel bedroom

Riva Surya Bangkok

23 Thanon Phra Arthit; tel: 0 2633 5000;
www.rivasuryabangkok.com; $$

Opened in 2012 on the river in Bangkok's
most culturally rich area, the Riva is close
to the National Museum and Grand Pal-
ace, but also on the edge of the Khao San
party zone. There's a bar, a pool, a fitness
centre, and the Babble & Rum café has
riverview garden seating.

The Siam

3/2 Thanon Khao; tel: 0 2206 6999; www.
thesiamhotel.com; $$$$

Another 2012 riverside opening, beside
the Krung Thon Bridge, the Siam has styl-
ish Art Deco rooms that are individually
designed with nods to historic Siam. Along
with artworks and antiques, each room
has a personal butler and free Wi-Fi. At the
top end is Connie's Cottage, a 100-year-
old wooden house that was brought from
Ayutthaya by Jim Thompson and his close
friend Connie Mangskau.

Chinatown

Grand China Hotel Bangkok

215 Thanon Yaowarat; tel: 0 2224 9977;
www.grandchina.com; $$

Smart rooms with good river and city
views are a major draw at this large hotel,
as is the revolving restaurant on the 25th
floor. Set amid the Chinatown bustle, it's
10 minutes to Old City sights by taxi, or on
foot to the ferry pier.

Shanghai Mansion

479–81 Thanon Yaowarat; tel: 0 2221 2121;
www.shanghaimansion.com; $$

A classy boutique hotel in a part of
town often written off as lacking in
decent lodgings. Rooms have lovely
over-the-top chinoiserie, four-poster
beds and vibrant hues, many reflect-
ing those in nearby market alleyways.
It is feng shui heaven with free internet
access and a spa.

Pathumwan

A-One Inn

25/13–15 Soi Kasemsan 1, Thanon Rama I;
tel: 0 2215 3029; www.aoneinn.com; $

Very basic rooms, but they do have sat-
ellite TV and air-conditioning, making it
a good price for an area so close to Siam
Square shops and the Skytrain. Internet
café with Wi-Fi, and a laundry service. It's
a popular spot, but there are other options
on the same street if it's full.

Grand Hyatt Erawan

494 Thanon Ratchadamri; tel: 0 2254 1234;
www.hyatt.com; $$$

This favourite with Thai socialites is
located beside the Erawan Shrine, so
perfect for downtown shopping. It has an
imposing formal lobby with huge classical
columns, an excellent range of restaurants and, in the basement, the night-
club-cum-restaurant Spasso.

InterContinental Bangkok

973 Thanon Ploenchit; tel: 0 2656 0444;
https://bangkok.intercontinental.com; $$$

Linked to Chit Lom Skytrain station
and Gaysorn Plaza mall, this hotel has

Lobby of the Grand Hyatt Erawan

spacious rooms with internet access and CD players. A rooftop swimming pool has fine city views, and there's a very cute Italian bistro, called Grossi, in the basement.

Siam Kempinski

991/9 Thanon Rama I; tel: 0 2162 9000; www. kempinski.com; $$$

This hotel is located just behind Siam Paragon mall. The rooms have garden views, flat screen TVs, iPod connectivity and broadband internet. Other facilities include Sra Bua molecular Thai restaurant and a branch of Copenhagen's Michelin-starred Kiin Kiin, which is standout, if you have the cash to afford it.

VIE Hotel

117/39–40 Thanon Phaya Thai; tel: 0 2309 3939; www.accorhotels.com; $$

This hotel has modern, elegant rooms fitted with LCD TVs, computers, Wi-Fi and lots of pleasant Asian design touches. It's just a few minutes' walk from downtown malls including MBK and Siam Paragon. There's a rooftop pool bar to relax at and a decent international restaurant, also with good views.

Sukhumvit

Ambassador

171 Sukhumvit Soi 11; tel: 0 2254 0444; www.ambassadorbkk.com; $$

The Ambassador is a huge, rather dated hotel, but it does have a spa, an outdoor pool and decent rooms in this price range, all of which have been recently renovated. It's only a 5-minute walk to Nana Skytrain station, and there are lots of good restaurants and clubs nearby.

The Atlanta Hotel

78 Sukhumvit Soi 2; tel: 0 2252 1650; www. theatlantahotelbangkok.com; $

A quirky 1950s throwback, this was Sukhumvit's first hotel. Rich in character, with an exquisite period interior, it also has a strong moral ethos that holds no truck with sex tourists and allows no visitors. Pitched at 'suitable' guests, it describes itself as 'untouched by post-modern primitivism'. There is a pool in landscaped gardens and a good Thai restaurant.

Dream Hotel

10 Sukhumvit Soi 15; tel: 0 2254 8500; www. dreambkk.com; $

Cutting-edge design is at the forefront of this unique glass-encased hotel with stylish restaurants, a cigar bar, club and Dalí-inspired lounge. Guest rooms come complete with 42-inch plasma TVs, iPod Nanos and a bar stocked with Veuve-Clicquot Champagne.

JW Marriott

4 Sukhumvit Soi 2; tel: 0 2656 7700; www. marriott.com; $$$

This classy five-star hotel is just around the corner from the risqué Nana Entertainment Plaza, but don't let that deter you. It has all the usual superior amenities, including a large fitness centre, efficient business facil-

Infinity pool at SO Sofitel Bangkok

ities and spacious, well-appointed rooms. As befits one of the city's top hotels, it has some of the best dining – at the New York Steakhouse (see page 113).

Metropole Bangkok

2802 Thanon New Petchaburi; tel: 0 2314 8555; www.metropolebangkok.com; $$

The Metropole juxtaposes classic architecture with wood and natural toned furnishings for a classy and competitively priced stay. The facilities onsite include a café and bar, a cold onsen bathhouse and a swimming pool. Wi-Fi is available throughout the building.

Seven

3/15 Sukhumvit Soi 31; tel: 0 1616 2636; www.sevenbangkok.com; $$

Seven is an ultra-cool hotel with bar, gallery and café. Exclusive in terms of size, it has just six rooms, each with its own colour scheme and cosmological meaning based on the Thai tradition of assigning colours to days of the week. The 7th Heaven Bar, sundeck and free Wi-Fi are other attractions.

Sheraton Grande Sukhumvit

250 Thanon Sukhumvit; tel: 0 2649 8888; www.marriott.com; $$$

A five-star property with first-rate facilities and spacious rooms with all the amenities you would expect. Well located for the metro, it also has a beautifully landscaped pool and an excellent spa and lounge.

Silom and Bangrak

Baan Saladaeng Boutique Guesthouse

69/3 Saladaeng Soi 3; tel: 0 2636 3038; www.baansaladaeng.com; $

A very tasteful budget operation, with just nine themed-decor rooms with names such as Neo Siam, Moroccan Suite and Pop Art Mania. Each has air-conditioning, TV and Wi-Fi. There's a small coffee bar, and it's a great location for transport, restaurants and nightlife.

Dusit Thani

946 Thanon Rama IV; tel: 0 2200 9999; www.dusit.com; $$

Ideally located across from Lumphini Park, near Patpong's nightlife, and beside MRT and Skytrain stations, this was Bangkok's first luxury hotel when it opened in the 1970s. Recent refurbishments have been made to the Asian-tinged interior. Enjoy a massage at the Devarana Spa, then float on to one of its 13 bars and restaurants, including top-floor D'Sens for impeccable French dining (see page 114).

Lebua at State Tower

State Tower; 1055/111 Thanon Silom; tel: 0 2624 9999; www.lebua.com; $$$

These luxury, contemporary Asian-style rooms and suites are housed in the 64-storey State Tower and have river or city view balconies. The opulent rooftop eating and drinking outlets are collectively called The Dome (see page 63) and include Sirocco (see page 116), Mezzaluna and Breeze, as well as the

Sheraton Grande Sukhumvit's spa

sophisticated Distil Bar, all with superb city and river views.

Mandarin Oriental Bangkok

48 Charoen Krung Soi 40; tel: 0 2659 9000; www.mandarinoriental.com; $$$$

Bangkok's riverside Grand Dame has been hosting guests since 1876; its original Authors' Wing still has period suites and a delightful tearoom. Newer wings attract a luminous guest list that includes royalty and stars in every field from parliament to pop. The excellent Le Normandie French restaurant requires a jacket for dinner, while the Oriental Spa offers East-meets-West themes. See also page 115.

Pullman Bangkok Hotel G

188 Thanon Silom; tel: 0 2352 4000; www. pullmanhotels.com; $$

This 38-storey hotel located in the quieter part of busy Thanon Silom is only a short walk to Chong Nonsi Skytrain station. Furnished in a chic modern style, it caters to both business and leisure travellers. Scarlett Wine Bar & Restaurant has stunning city views from its 37th-floor perch.

La Residence

173/8–9 Thanon Surawong; tel: 0 2266 5400; www.laresidencebangkok.com; $

A small hotel with a friendly vibe and funky, individually decorated rooms of different sizes. It is a short cab ride to Thanon Silom, with the attractions of Patpong night market, restaurants and pubs, and also to the river, from where there are boats to many city highlights. Rooms

include two modest suites, one with garden balcony views. All accommodation has Wi-Fi access.

SO Sofitel Bangkok

2 Thanon Sathorn Nua; tel: 0 2624 0000; www.sofitel.com; $$$

So Sofitel comes packaged with lots of youthful elegance, from the chocolate 'lab' by the entrance to the semi-alfresco Park Society bar-restaurant with great city views across Lumphini Park. The rooms have a five elements theme of Water, Earth, Wood, Metal and Fire, all from a different designer, and have Apple Mac-minis. Christian Lacroix designed the uniforms.

The Sukhothai

13/3 Thanon Sathorn Thai; tel: 0 2344 8888; www.sukhothai.com; $$$

Drawing architectural inspiration from the ancient Siamese kingdom of Sukhothai, this place was years ahead of the pack in its use of Asian detailing in a contemporary setting. Well-appointed rooms are in tropical gardens, with a beautiful infinity pool. Facilities include the stylish Italian restaurant La Scala; one of Bangkok's best up-market Thai restaurants, Celadon; and the tastefully attired Zuk Bar.

Take a Nap Hostel

920–6 Thanon Rama 4; tel: 0 2637 0015; www.takeanaphotel.com; $

Take a Nap has basic but attractive rooms, each with an artistic theme, such as Japanese waves, Pop Art, and the child-like Happy Forest, painted on

Somerset Maugham suite at the Mandarin Oriental

the wall. There is air-conditioning and a few TV stations available, but no fridges or wardrobes. It is close to the Patpong night market and just a five-minute walk to Skytrain and subway stations.

W Bangkok
106 Thanon Sathorn Nua; tel: 0 2344 4000; www.whotels.com; $$$

The luxury W chain has its Bangkok flagship right beside Chong Nonsi Skytrain station, in the middle of the rapidly developing business district. The colour scheme includes lots of purple, silver and black, and rooms have iPad docking to link with TV screens. The casual all-day restaurant does international food. The pool has underwater lighting and speakers.

West of Bangkok

Baan Sukchoke Country Resort
103 Moo 5 Damnoen Saduak; tel: 032 254 301; $

There is a pleasing feel to these simple but clean wooden bungalows arranged around a canal. The surroundings are like an informal open-air museum with traditional boats and farming equipment scattered around. The alfresco café serves decent Thai food. You can also arrange to visit the local floating market by boat from here.

Kanchanaburi

Apple's Retreat & Guest House
153/4 Moo 4 Sutjai Bridge; tel: 0 3451 2017/3457; www.applenoikanchanaburi. com; $

This friendly and well-run place has quiet, simple bungalows in gardens beside the river. It is locally famous for its good food and Thai cooking courses. The guesthouse also runs a tour company that specialises in bicycle trips around the province's national parks.

River Kwai Jungle Rafts
Baan Tahsao, Amphur Saiyoke; tel: 08 1734 0667 or 0 2642 5497 (Bangkok office); www. serenatahotels.com; $$

These river raft rooms are 100km (62 miles) from town, and a good choice if you want to explore the surrounding countryside. There's a floating restaurant and bar, and guests can swim, fish and visit nearby ethnic tribal villages. No electricity at night.

Ayutthaya

AllSum Hostel
50/1 Soi Bua Wan; tel: 0 2747 5013; $

This is a popular tourist hostel in town, located only 10 minutes' walk away from the main sights of Ayutthaya and offering reasonably clean rooms and modern facilities. Dorm beds come in rooms holding six to eight people, with mixed or female only rooms available. Social spaces include a terrace, garden and common room.

iuDia
11-12 U-Tong Road, Moo 4, Pratuchai; tel: 08 6080 1888; www.iudia.com; $$

The furnishings in these very smart rooms are modern, while drawing on traditional

Traditional meets the contemporary at The Sukhothai

motifs for inspiration. iuDia is right on the river, close to the Old City ruins (there are views from the hotel), and they will provide bicycles on request. This is a refreshingly chic option for Ayutthaya.

Phetchaburi

Fisherman's Resort

170 Moo 1, Hat Chao Samran; tel: 0 3244 1370; www.thefishermansresort.com; $$

This boutique resort is 15km (10m) from town on the beach at Hat Chao Samran, and promotes the merits of its undeveloped location as an alternative to Hua Hin. Built in classic Asian style, it has a pool, a spa and a beachfront restaurant serving Thai and western food.

Rabieng Rim Nam Guesthouse

1 Thanon Chisa-In; tel: 0 3242 5707; $

This popular backpacker haunt is centrally located beside a busy bridge over the river. It's cheap but has small box-like rooms and shared bathrooms. Also has a good restaurant.

Hua Hin

Baan Talay Dao

2/10 Soi Takiab; tel: 0 2751 6854; www. baantalaydao.com; $$

The 'House Between the Sea and Stars' is a resort built around a 90-year-old teak house on the road towards Khao Takiab. The accommodation is mainly studio rooms, but there are also several pleasant villas and suites arranged around a pool and jacuzzi area. Garden pathways lead past small water features to the beach.

The restaurant serves both Thai and international food.

Centara Grand Beach Resort & Villas

1 Damnernkasem Road; tel: 0 3251 2021; www.centarahotelsresorts.com; $$$

This gorgeous hotel retains the white colonial elegance from the 1920s when it was built to house distinguished guests at the newly created royal retreat of Hua Hin. Lush gardens are the backdrop for a choice of villas or handsome rooms, while infinity pools offer prime sunbathing spots by the beach.

Pattaya

InterContinental Pattaya Resort

437 Thanon Phra Tamnak; tel: 0 3825 9888; www.ighg.com; $$$

In a secluded spot on the Phra Tamnak headland, this beautifully landscaped resort has calming water elements and its own beach. Many of the rooms have their own ocean-facing *sala* (pavilion), and the Amburaya Spa is there for body tuning.

Rabbit Resort

Dongtan Beach, Jomtien; tel: 0 3825 1730; $$

This beach resort had local village sensibilities in mind when it designed cosy Thai-style houses and bungalows amid pretty palm-tree gardens. Villa accommodation is also available, with two en suite bedrooms. All options are individually decorated with original artworks and antiques. Two pools, a restaurant and an ocean-side grill.

Street restaurant

RESTAURANTS

Bangkok's dining options are wonderfully varied. There is tasty Thai street food served at plastic tables for as little as 20 baht a dish; tiny cafés galore; riverside garden diners; and luxury roof-top restaurants, where you can blow thousands. The city now has two branches of Thai restaurants with Michelin star connections, while international options include French, Italian, Chinese, Japanese, Indian, Mexican and a whole host of others.

Most Thai meals have dishes placed in the middle of the table to be shared by all; the larger the group, the more dishes you can try. Put a helping of rice onto your plate, together with small portions of various dishes at the side. You will usually get a spoon and fork as utensils. Use the fork to push food onto the spoon. Chopsticks are used only for Chinese and noodle dishes.

Condiments on the table usually include dried ground red chilli; sliced chilli with vinegar; sliced chilli with *nam pla* (fish sauce); and white sugar. These are mainly used to add extra flavour to noodle dishes.

The more expensive restaurants add a service charge of 10 percent, otherwise, although tipping is not customary it is usual to leave the small change left over from the bill.

To combine a Thai dinner with sightseeing on a cruise along the Chao Phraya River, contact Yok Yor (www.yokyor.co.th) or Manohra Cruises (tel: 0 2476 0022; www.manohracruises.com).

Dusit

Chon Thai

The Siam hotel, 3/2 Thanon Khao; tel: 0 2206 6999; www.thesiamhotel.com; daily noon–11pm; $$$

This riverside Thai restaurant is in a beautifully preserved traditional wooden house decorated with antiques. The small, home-style menu has well executed versions of classics from pomelo salad to crab red curry. The hotel shuttle boat leaves Taksin Pier regularly until 6.30pm and can be arranged by phone to stop at piers along the way.

Kaloang Home Kitchen

2 Thanon Sri Ayutthaya; tel: 0 2281 9228; daily 11am–10pm; $$

Located behind the National Library where Thanon Sri Ayutthaya ends amid riverbank boatyards, rustic Kaloang

A meal for one person, excluding drinks and taxes:
$$$$ = more than B1,500
$$$ = B700–1,500
$$ = B200–700
$ = less than B200

serves good Thai standards, particularly grilled fish and seafood such as curried crab.

Chinatown

Soi Texas

Soi Padung Dao; 9am–2am; $$

Famed for its food, this small Chinatown lane is named after the Texas Suki restaurant 50m/yds on the right. It also has two packed stalls at the mouth of the *soi*, Rut and Lek and T & K (open from 6pm). They serve great curried crab and seafood that is superb charcoal-grilled or fried with garlic and chilli.

Thai Heng

50 metres/yds into Yaowarat Soi 8, opposite Wat Bamphen Chin Phrot; tel: 0 2222 6791; Mon–Sat 10am–5pm; $

An 80-year-old café that some say makes the best Hainan chicken rice in Chinatown. Simple but delicious, it is chicken on rice soaked in chicken fat, served with spicy *nam jim* dip. It is also famed for Hainan *sukiyaki*: meat and veg in a peppery broth.

Yim Yim

89 Thanon Padsai; tel: 0 2224 2203; daily 11am–2pm, 5–10pm; $$

Old-style Chinese family restaurant with six tables nestled amid the household clutter. This is a Chinatown institution famed for crab claws baked in a clay pot and Chinese sashimi, which comes with vegetables and sweet sesame sauce.

Pathumwan

Crêpes & Co

59/4 Langsuan Soi 1; tel: 0 2015 3388; https://crepesand.co; daily 9am–11pm; $$

A relaxed and reliable crêperie that specialises in unusual international fillings along with the crêpe suzettes. It also serves tajines, *briouattes* and other Moroccan dishes, plus Greek favourites like *melizana salata*. The spacious open plan room has thick, blond wood pillars and beams, and sofas and armchairs in the centre to lend a living room ambience. There is a popular Sunday brunch on offer, too.

Gaggan

68/1 Soi Langsuan; tel: 0 2652 1700; www.eatatgaggan.com; daily 5.30–11.30pm; $$$

In a summer-house interior of white woods and rattan this 'progressive Indian' has El Bulli-inspired molecular cooking techniques in dishes like roasted foie gras with raspberry chutney. It's inventive and excellent, and the traditional fare such as *bhunna* mutton curry is as good as you'll taste anywhere. The small roof terrace is a good spot for pre- or post-dinner drinks.

Gai Tort Soi Polo

137/1–2 Soi Polo, Thanon Witthayu; tel: 0 2252 2252; daily 7am–7pm; $

One of Bangkok's most famous fried chicken shops. The *gai* is marinated in soy sauce, tamarind and pepper,

and served piping hot and topped with fried garlic. Eat it with *som tam* (green papaya salad) and dipped in sweet-and-spicy and sour-and-spicy sauces.

Greyhound Café

2nd floor, Central World, 4/1-2 Thanon Ratchadamri; tel: 0 2613 1263; www.greyhoundcafe.co.th; Sat–Thu 11am–10pm, Fri until 11pm; $$$

Part of a larger Thai brand that started out in fashion before expanding to fill bellies as well, this popular café has an extensive menu offering noodle dishes and Thai classics like crab meat on fried rice, as well as an excellent selection of dishes for vegetarians, including pad thai and fettuccini with grilled vegetables.

Hyde & Seek

65/1 Athenée Residence, Soi Ruamrudee; tel: 0 2168 5152; www.hydeandseek.com; daily 11.30am–10pm; $$$

A stylish gastro-bar with custom cocktails and upmarket European meals. Try baby back ribs glazed with chocolate and chilli, or seabass with melted cabbage and shellfish emulsion. Eat inside or enjoy the garden terrace.

La Monita Taqueria

888/26 Mahatun Plaza, Thanon Ploenchit; tel: 0 2650 9581; www.lamonita.com; daily 11.30am–10pm; $$

Small Mexican diner with cheap decor, good food and a friendly atmosphere. All the usual burritos, nachos, wings and Mexi or Cali tacos to wash down with mojitos and beer, plus good smoky guacamole and free corkage.

El Osito

888/23-24 Mahatun Plaza, Thanon Ploenchit; tel: 0 2651 4399; http://ositobkk.com; Mon–Sat 5–11.30pm; $$

Spanish diner meets New York deli amid polished concrete walls, exposed wires and bare bulbs hung from the ceiling. The daytime menu of sandwiches, such as Reuben and homemade pastrami, at night morphs into Spanish drinking, snacks and full meals including grilled rib-eye and prawns with fried parsley, olive oil, garlic, and crispy French bread. Good bottled beers and cider are alternatives to wine.

The Rain Tree Café

61 Wireless Rd; tel: 0 2650 8800; www.marriott.com; daily 6–10.30am, noon–2.30pm and 6–10.30pm; $$$

Modern, lively Thai furnishings set a classy yet laid-back tone for this all-you-can-eat buffet restaurant in the Athenee Hotel. This is up-scale buffet dining, with chefs making five separate dishes daily, along with a host of sides, sushi and other delicacies. Dress is smart-casual; advance reservations are a must.

Sra Bua by Kiin Kiin

Siam Kempinski Hotel, Thanon 991/9 Rama I; tel: 0 2162 9000; www.

Perusing the menu at a Japanese restaurant

srabuabykiinkiin.com/en; daily noon–3pm, 6pm–midnight; $$$$

This outlet of Copenhagen's Michelin-starred Kiin Kiin has a rather masculine, businesslike interior, but displays a thrilling modern slant on Thai food with dishes such as green curry mousse, *tom klong* soup served as jellies, and red curry ice cream.

Theo Mio

InterContinental Bangkok, 973 Thanon Ploenchit; tel: 0 2656 0444; https://bangkok.intercontinental.com; Mon–Fri 11.30am–11.30pm, Sat–Sun 11.30am–2pm; $$$

The trattoria style of chef Theo Randall, it has an elegant deli ambience. There's a floor of large black and white checks, marble counter displays of wines, bread and cold meats, and a menu that eschews obvious Italian exports for dishes such as *burrata* salad with anchovies and pressed beef with chocolate and orange zest.

Zuma

St Regis Hotel, 159 Thanon Ratchadamri; tel: 0 2252 4707; www.zumarestaurant.com; Mon–Sat L & D; 11.30am–1am; $$$$

This branch of London's modern Japanese restaurant is all natural woods and granite with an electro background. The great-quality produce includes hot, cold and sparkling sakes and dishes including miso-marinated black cod. The bar extends through full wall windows to a split level garden with sofas.

Sukhumvit

Akbar

¼ Sukhumvit Soi 3; tel: 0 2255 6935; daily 10.30am–midnight; $$

One of the oldest Indian restaurants in Bangkok, it serves reliable tandooris, vindaloos and kormas, on two floors charmingly decorated like an over-the-top curio shop, with Arabic lanterns, Indian rugs and fairy lights.

Bo.lan

42 Soi Pichai Ronnarong, Sukhumvit Soi 26; tel: 0 2260 2962; www.bolan.co.th; Tue–Sun 6–10.30pm; $$$

Bo and Dylan set up this townhouse operation fresh from working at London's Michelin-starred Thai restaurant Naam, and have a similar focus on traditional recipes. The short menu starts with a herb liquor, *ya dong*, and continues through regional flavours in dishes including sweet cured pork in coconut cream and deep-fried fish with an eye-watering, spicy-sour dipping sauce.

Broccoli Revolution

899 Sukhumvit Soi; tel: 0 2662 5001; http://broccolirevolution.com; Mon–Fri 9am–10pm, Sat–Sun 7am–10pm; $$

With an emphasis on vegan cuisine, Broccoli Revolution is an excellent option for anybody wishing to avoid the meat-heavy options on most other restaurant menus. The dishes presented to diners are derived from a global mix of recipes, while ingredients are fresh

An exquisite pistachio dessert

and locally-sourced. The juice bar here is also worth checking out.

Enoteca

39 Sukhumvit Soi 27; tel: 0 2258 4386; www.enotecabangkok.com; daily 6–10.30pm; $$$

A very good menu in a small place with exposed brickwork, blackboard menu and arty posters. Saffron risotto flecked with liquorice, suckling pig with coffee-laced chestnut purée, and chocolate foam on rum-seasoned crushed ice are typically clever touches.

Govinda

6/5/6 Sukhumvit Soi 22; tel: 0 2663 4970; www.govindarestaurantbkk.com; Wed–Mon noon–3pm and 6–10.30pm; $$

All-vegetarian Italian food that includes a variety of pastas, thin-crust pizzas, risottos and bakes. Desserts such as tiramisu and cheesecake are egg-free. Also serves bread and ice cream made on the premises, and imported beers.

Jang Won

202/9–19 Sukhumvit Plaza, corner Sukhumvit Soi 12; tel: 0 2251 2636; daily 9am–11pm; $$

One of many Korean cafés in this plaza. Diners sit in family-sized booths to enjoy Seoul food such as *ugeoji haejangguk* (spicy beef and vegetable soup), *dolsot bibimbap* (rice and beef cooked in hot stone pots) and sizzling *bulgogi* beef.

Krua Rommai

29 Sukhumvit Soi 38; tel: 0 2713 6048/9; www.facebars.com; daily 11.30am–2.30pm, 6–10.30pm; $$$

Tasty authentic Thai fare, such as lobster salad with whole shrimps, tom yam seafood, and grilled chicken, is served up in a rustic setting. The covered seating area is surrounded by plants and, at night, lit by lanterns, giving it a pleasant ambience.

Long Table

Floor 25, The Column Residence, Sukhumvit Soi 16; tel: 0 2302 2557/9; www.longtablebangkok.com; daily 5pm–2am; $$$

Fantastic city views and a long table for communal-style dining are the focal points for this classy modern Thai restaurant. It has panache, both in interior decor and dishes such as crab in yellow curry and foie gras with tamarind, which are both hits from a menu served Western-style in individual portions.

Nasir Al-Masri

4/6 Sukhumvit Soi 3/1; tel: 0 2253 5582; www.restaurant-shishah-nasir.com; daily 24 hours; $

This area is often called Soi Arab because of its Middle Eastern operations selling kebabs and Lebanese-style dips. Along with the standard skewers, 'Nasir the Egyptian' also has specialities from home, such as *fuul* (mashed beans in oil) and

Thai peppers   *Nahm*

molokhaya (a spinach-like vegetable mixed with garlic). Outside, men smoke shiny metal shisha pipes, just like in downtown Cairo.

New York Steakhouse

JW Marriott, 4 Sukhumvit Soi 2; tel: 0 2656 7700; www.marriott.com; daily 6–11pm; $$$$

A top-notch restaurant with a relaxed atmosphere despite the formal trappings of club-like dark woods and high-backed leather chairs. Good Manhattan clam chowder sets up the grain-fed Angus beef, sliced at the table from a silver trolley (the beef is imported chilled, not frozen). There's a long Martini list and fine wines, and atmospheric black-and-white photos of the Big Apple adorn the walls. Booking is essential.

Opposite Mess Hall

27/1 Sukhumvit Soi 51; tel: 0 2662 6330; www.oppositebangkok.com; Tue–Sun 7pm–1am; $$

Helmed by the popular chef Jess Barnes, this is the dining operation of the art bar WTF, opposite. It's a small venue, with a working men's vibe and simple Aussie-Euro food that's big on comforting dishes such as smoked bone marrow dumplings with beef broth, pumpkin and fermented daikon. Or try the steamed Chinese buns with fried tempeh, kimchi, sriracha mayo and scamorza cheese. It's tasty stuff and great with a beer.

Philippe Restaurant

20/15–17 Sukhumvit Soi 39; tel: 0 2259 4577/8; www.philipperestaurant.com; daily 11.30am–2.30pm and 6.30–10.30pm; $$$

Small restaurant with very good classic French fare. The mini grand staircase sweeping from the mezzanine and nicotine colour scheme make a comfortable setting for delicious roast lamb loin with duck liver sauce or trout with lemon butter and almond.

Pizzeria Limoncello

17 Sukhumvit Soi 11; tel: 0 2651 0707; www.zanottigroup.com; daily noon–2pm and 6–11pm; $$

There are some Italian standards on the menu, but most people come for the big tasty pizzas prepared in the wood-fired oven. The summery lemon-and-blue interior with ceiling frescoes of cherubs amid wispy clouds is a cheery setting for fun dining. The restaurant has the signature buzz of owner Zanotti. It's often full, so book ahead.

Quince

14/2 Soi Somkid; tel: 0 4868 2639; www.quincebangkok.com; daily 6pm–midnight; $$$

Trendy European restaurant with earthy farmhouse presentation and a commitment to local produce where possible. They're good on fresh salads such as blueberry beetroot with feta cheese and rocket, and homely international fare, including chicken tag-

Tom Yam Gung

ine-style with lemon and chickpeas. There's a buzzy, pub-like atmosphere, occasional DJs, arty cocktails and a good wine list.

Ruen Mallika

189 Sukhumvit Soi 22; tel: 0 2663 3211-2; www.ruenmallika.com; daily noon–11pm; $$

Rama I-period wooden house with garden tables and traditional floor-cushion seating inside. Options include *kaeng tai pla* (pungent southern-style fish-stomach curry), which tastes better than it sounds, *mee krob* (sweet, herby crispy noodles) and deep-fried flowers.

Soi 38 Food Stalls

Sukhumvit Soi 38; daily 5pm–1am; $

The mix of rough-and-tumble food stalls at the entrance of this *soi* is one of the city's most famous street-food areas, and is ideally placed to fill up after a night in the Thonglor bars opposite. Try rice gruel, spring rolls, spicy crab salad, crispy pork, *nam kaeng sai* (desserts with ice) and countless others. Wash them down with fruit juice or beer.

Vientiane Kitchen

8 Sukhumvit Soi 36; tel: 0 2258 6171; www.vientiane-kitchenbkk.com; daily noon–midnight; $$

Lao–Isaan food in a *sala* (pavilion) complex where musicians play traditional music under trees laden with fairy lights. This is a fun dining experience, with rice whisky, spicy salads, grilled marinated chicken and countryside favourites such as *kai mot daeng* (red-ant eggs).

Aoi

132/10–11 Silom Soi 6; tel: 0 2235 2321–2; www.aoi-bkk.com; daily 11.30am–2pm and 5.30–10pm; $$$

Black stone walkways give a cool calm to this unfussy restaurant serving excellent Japanese food. Downstairs is a sushi bar, with two floors of private and semi-private rooms above (available at a surcharge). Set meals are much cheaper than ordering à la carte. There is another branch in Emporium shopping mall.

The China House

Mandarin Oriental, 48 Charoen Krung Soi 40; tel: 0 2659 9000; www.mandarinoriental.com; daily 11.30am–2.30pm and 6–10.30pm; $$$

The beautiful 1930s Shanghainese Art Deco interior features red lanterns, carved wood and ebony pillars. Miniature black-and-white photos and Chinese calligraphy cover the walls; a brass samovar steams in the central tearoom. It's a wonderful setting for top-quality dishes including hot-and-sour soup with fresh herbs and sweet lobster meat, or hand-pulled noodles with green crab claw.

Eat Me

1/F, 1/6 Piphat Soi 2, off Thanon Convent;

Cooking traditional dishes

tel: 0 2238 0931; www.eatmerestaurant.com; daily 3pm–1am; $$$

An extremely popular Australian-run restaurant, often exhibiting the work of edgy young artists from the nearby H Gallery. The modern eclectic menu features dishes such as charred scallops with mango, herb salad, pickled onions and citrus dressing. Low lighting and a fragmented layout lend a sense of intimacy. On pleasantly cool nights ask for a table on the terrace. There is a decent wine list.

Harmonique

22 Charoen Krung Soi 34; tel: 0 2237 8175; Mon–Sat 11am–10pm; $$

This cute restaurant occupies several old Chinese shophouses and spills into leafy courtyards. Due to a large contingent of Western diners, the spices are too quiet for many Thais, but the curries and spicy salads are generally tasty. It is a relaxing place to hang out, if you want an 'out of town' ambience, and is very handy for the riverside hotels.

Issaya Siamese Club

4 Soi Sri Aksorn, Chua Ploeng Rd; tel: 0 2787 8768; www.issaya.com; $$$$

Thailand's most famous home-grown chef, Ian Kittichai has restaurants in Europe and the US. This is his signature Bangkok outlet, located in a beautiful 100-year-old wooden house, where he serves modern Thai interpretations. Typical is the red chilli-glazed

baby back ribs infused with *tom yum* broth.

Krua Aroy Aroy

4 Thanon Pan, Silom; tel: 0 2635 2365; daily 10am–6pm; $

Opposite Maha Uma Devi Temple, with a sign reading 'Delicious, Delicious, Delicious', this wooden-stool café features regional dishes. Curries include *nam ya ka ti* (minced fish in coconut milk), and noodles come deep-fried (*mee krob*) and cold (*khanom jeen*).

Nahm

Metropolitan Hotel, 27 Thanon Sathorn Tai; tel: 0 2625 3333; www.comohotels.com/metropolitanbangkok; daily noon–2pm, 6.30–10.30pm; $$$$

This is a branch of what was Europe's first Michelin-starred Thai restaurant, run by Australian chef David Thompson. The ultra-traditional menu tours the regions and includes intriguing flavour blends including northern pork, prawn and tamarind relish served with braised mackerel, sweet pork, crispy acacia and soft boiled eggs. Sit inside or by the outdoor pool.

Le Normandie

Mandarin Oriental, 48 Charoen Krung Soi 40; tel: 0 2236 0400; www.mandarinoriental.com; Mon–Sat noon–2.30pm, daily 7–10.30pm; $$$$

It's all about formal French dining with concoctions such as smoked eel (with eel mousse and caviar on beetroot carpaccio) and goose liver with Périgord

Grilled squid

truffles that verge on brilliance. In the stately marmalade-coloured interior, crystal chandeliers hang from a quilted silk ceiling, while full-length windows overlook the Chao Phraya River. Top-notch wine list and quiet piano music. Jackets required.

Sirocco

63/F, Lebua at State Tower, 1055/111 Thanon Silom; tel: 0 2624 9555; www. thedomebkk.com; daily 6pm–1am; $$$$
This spectacular 200m (656ft) -high rooftop restaurant has a breathtaking panorama of the river. The striking Greco-Roman architecture and resident jazz band add to the sense of occasion. (The Greco-Roman setting may seem incongruous, but Euro-Asian architecture has a pedigree stretching back over a century and is, in fact, very Bangkok.) On one side there is spot-lit garden landscaping and a sweeping staircase with a jazz band at the top, on the other a sheer drop to the street below. The Mediterranean food can be inconsistent, but is often excellent. Also part of The Dome complex: classy Distil Bar has good seafood; stylish Mezzaluna offers Italian cuisine; and Breeze serves an enticing modern Asian menu. Great for a memorable splash-out meal.

Somboon Seafood

169/7–11 Thanon Surawong; tel: 0 2233 3104; www.somboonseafood.com; daily 4–11.30pm; $$$
Come to this no-frills café outlet on four floors, with tubular metal furniture, for excellent Chinese-style seafood. Curried crabs and prawns devoured with spicy *nam jim* dipping sauce are favourites, along with whole fish cooked every which way. The canteen-like service won't win awards, but the food just might.

Somtum Der Saladaeng

5/5 Thanon Saladaeng; tel: 0 2632 4499; www.somtumder.com; daily 11am–2.30pm and 4.30–10.30pm; $$
Set inside a crisp minimalist space, Somtum Der is a great place to try out the kind of Isan cooking common to northern Thailand. Dishes will be slightly saltier than those you might find elsewhere in the country. Classics include *som tam* green papaya salad and tom yum soup. Lots of spicy dishes dominate the menu.

Tamil Nadu

Silom Soi 11; tel: 0 2235 6336; daily 8.30am–10pm; $
Basic café serving the south Indian community close to Bangkok's most ornate Indian temple. The speciality is *masala dosa*, a pancake made of rice flour and *urad dal*, stuffed with potato and onion curry and served with coconut chutney.

Zanotti

G/F, Saladaeng Colonnade, 21/2 Soi Sala Daeng; tel: 0 2636 0002; www. zanottigroup.com; daily 11.30am–2pm and 6–10.30pm; $$$

Rooftop setting of Sirocco

Thai-style mussels

Chef-owner Gianmaria Zanotti has created a restaurant that people visit for the buzz as much as the food. The Italian fare includes more than 20 pasta dishes and quality seafood and steaks charcoal-grilled over orange wood from Chiang Mai in the north of Thailand. A good selection of wines is offered by the glass. The chic wine bar Vino di Zanotti opposite also serves a full menu and has live jazz.

Banglamphu

May Kaidee

117/1 Thanon Tanao; tel: 0 2281 7137; www.maykaidee.com; daily 9am–11pm; $

May has a sound reputation for her vegetarian Thai standards. Northeastern dishes (with mushrooms, tofu and soya beans) and *massaman* curry (with tofu, potatoes and peanuts) are popular selections. Loved your meal? Learn how to cook it by booking one of May's cooking lessons. To find this place, take the street next to Burger King and turn left. There is a second outlet 50m/yds away and another at 33 Thanon Samsen.

Pen Thai Food

229 Soi Rambuttri (pier Phra Athit); tel: 0 2282 2320; daily 7am–7.30pm; $

Khun Sitichai has had this spot since 1980, long before the first backpackers arrived. His menu has changed little. The spicy catfish curry, soups and deep-fried fish are still displayed outside in metal pots and trays in street-stall fashion and there are a few tables

to sit at. And at B20–40 per dish, the prices haven't changed much either.

Thip Samai

313 Thanon Maha Chai; tel: 0 2226 6666; https://thipsamai.com; daily 5pm–2am; $

Located close to the Golden Mount, this is a very basic but legendary café that does several versions (and nothing else) of pad thai, fried noodles with dried shrimps, roasted peanuts and bean sprouts, that is often claimed as Thailand's national dish. Options run from the traditional to 'Superb', made with fresh prawns and wrapped in a fried-egg casing.

Kanchanaburi

Keeree Tara Restaurant

43/1 River Kwai Road; tel: 0 3451 3855; daily 11am–11pm; $$

A stylish boutique restaurant with mock Sukhothai-era pillars and detailing. Sit on the atmospheric riverside terraces and enjoy a range of dishes including the speciality: snakefish with spicy salad.

Hua Hin

Brasserie de Paris

3 Naresdamri Road; tel: 0 9900 27235; www.brasseriedeparis.net; 10.30am–10pm; $$$

Sit upstairs at this wooden pier restaurant for views of fishing boats bobbing on the waves. It has delicious freshly caught seafood served French-style, such as rock lobster *au beurre blanc*.

Preparing for a puppet show

NIGHTLIFE

Bangkok's nightlife scene is large and varied, running from itinerant beer bars in the back of camper vans to hi-tech dance clubs and sophisticated cocktail venues with breathtaking views. Live music includes ska, jazz, blues and pop, plus a good opera company, while theatre takes in contemporary dance, traditional puppetry and the world-famous ladyboy cabaret. Good places to hang out are Thanons Khao San, Ratchadaphisek, Sukhumvit, Silom and the busy lanes of Soi Thonglor. Silom Sois 2 and 4 have lively gay-oriented options. Below is a selection of the most celebrated venues.

Music, theatre and cabaret

Ad Here the 13th Blues Bar
13 Thanon Samsen; tel: 08-9769-4613
Musicians turn up to jam blues and jazz in this tiny bar close to Khao San Road. There's a laid-back vibe and a mix of Thai and Western clients.

Calypso Cabaret
Asiatique Thanon Charoenkrung (between Sois 72–76); tel: 0 2688 1415-7; www.calypsocabaret.com
One of the city's best *katoey* (transsexual) cabarets performed by sequinned artistes who have gone through various stages of sex-change. Shows include anything from Marilyn Monroe impersonators to Thai classical dance.

Joe Louis Theatre
Asiatique, Charoen Krung Sois 72–76; tel: 0 2688 3322; www.joelouistheatre.com
This theatre is responsible for reviving the fading art of *hun lakhon lek*, a unique form of Thai puppetry. Three puppeteers move on stage manipulating expressive marionettes. One show nightly at 8pm.

Sala Chalerm Krung Theatre
66 Thanon Charoen Krung; tel: 0 2224 4499; www.salachalermkrung.com
See Thai classical theatre here as it hosts *khon* masked drama performances on Friday and Saturday from 7pm. It's unusual to see this in a theatre; most shows are in hotels or themed tourist spots.

Siam Niramit
19 Thanon Tiamruammit; tel: 0 2649 9222; www.siamniramit.com
A beautifully costumed extravaganza that traverses the country's history and diverse cultures in three acts. Nightly performance at 8pm. Preshow buffet dinner is served.

Tawandang German Brewery
462/61 Thanon Rama III; tel: 0 2678 1114; www.tawandang.com

Dance show accompanying dinner at the Mandarin Oriental

Not a German brewery (although they have German beers and food) but a pub-cum-theatre with an eclectic programme of Thai-Western music and cabaret. House band, costumed dancers, magic acts and even ballet.

Thailand Cultural Centre
Thanon Ratchadaphisek; tel: 0 2247 0028
Poor acoustics but it's one of the few places to stage performances by the Bangkok Opera and Symphony Orchestras. Also has pop, rock and jazz concerts and is the main venue for the International Festival of Dance and Music (Sept).

Bars and pubs

Apoteka Sukhumvit Soi 11
33 Sukhumvit Soi 11; tel: 0 9889 63639; www.apotekasoi11.com
Live music features heavily at this easy-going gastropub, which is ranged over two floors, including a balcony with views of the stage.

The Club at Koi
Fl 39 & 40 Sathorn Square Building, Thanon Narathiwat; tel: 0 2108 2005; https://theclubatkoi.com
The Singapore nightlife brand with multiple venues, including modern Asian cuisine at one of three restaurants, several bars and a club with top DJs and a cutting-edge sound system. Spectacular views.

DEMO
Thonglor Soi 10; tel: 0 2711 6970

Graffiti-covered walls create an urban warehouse ambience at this hot spot. Plays house music in all its forms and serves a long list of drinks. Great sound system, mock-classical French furniture and a very cool crowd.

Iron Fairies
394 Soi Thonglor (Sukhumvit Soi 55); tel: 0 2714 8875; www.theironfairies.com
One of the cutest of Thonglor's many bars, this tiny place is modelled as a foundry making iron fairy characters from the owner's books by day, and is full of old sewing machines, potion jars and iron machinery. At night it's a bar with absinthe, burgers and live jazz.

Maggie Choo's
320 Thanon Silom; tel: 0 1772 2144; https://maggiechoos.com
A fantasy 1930s' Shanghai bordello, Maggie's has an evocative period noodle shop, and beyond that, a large room modelled on a colonial-era bank vault. Leather couches, busts of Queen Victoria, dry ice and girls in slit-to-the-thigh Chinese dresses complete the picture.

Saxophone Pub
3/8 Thanon Phaya Thai; tel: 0 2246 5472; www.saxophonepub.com
The mainly Thai crowd enjoys a pubby atmosphere and balcony views at this lively two-floor venue. Some of the best jazz, R&B, soul and funk in town.

Lotus flowers are used as prayer offerings

A–Z

A

Addresses

Given the size of the city and its twisting alleyways, finding your way around can be confusing. Main roads often have smaller streets – called *sois* – leading off them, each having the main road's name followed by a number. For example, Thanon Sukhumvit (Sukhumvit Road) has side streets called Sukhumvit Soi 1, Sukhumvit Soi 3, etc., running in sequence, with odd and even numbers found on opposite sides of the road. *Sois* may be subdivided using a slash after the number followed by another number. The same system is used for shop and house addresses, a slash separating the block or building number from the shop. So an address might read 36/1 Sukhumvit 33/1.

Confusingly, the roads can have as many as four names, based on local usage, often reflecting the most important building in each. Street names are usually written in Thai and English, and most hotels provide business cards with the address written in Thai, to show taxi drivers. In tourist areas street names are often given in English, for example, Naklua Road. Not only do some streets have several different names, but with no standard transliterated English spellings for the Thai language, it is common to find a street or area spelt with several variants and broken or joined syllables.

B

Budgeting

Despite spiralling prices, by Western standards Bangkok is a bargain. Budget accommodation can be as cheap as B200 a night, with a delicious street-side meal and beer around B120. Five-star hotels cost from B5,000 (and with increasing competition, will often have even cheaper deals), while a three-course meal may be had for B1,000 without drinks (although wine is expensive, and one bottle will at least double that price). Refreshments in bars start around B60, and even in posh clubs they may be as little as B200. Bus fares cost B7–22, a Skytrain or metro ride B16–40 and taxi meters start at B35. If you live frugally, you can get by on B500 a day. But the sky is the limit here if you want to live it up at luxury hotels and eat at fine-dining restaurants.

Business hours

Government offices operate Mon–Fri 8.30am–4.30pm, most businesses Mon–Fri 8am–5.30pm (some also Sat 8.30am–noon) and banks Mon–Fri 9.30am–3.30pm. Money-changing kiosks are open daily until 8pm.

Shops generally open 10am–8pm, with some variations depending on loca-

On the bumper cars　　　　　　　　　*Suvarnabhumi Airport*

tion and the type of business. Department stores open daily 10.30am–9pm or 10pm.

Small open-air coffee shops and traditional Thai restaurants open at 7am and close at 8.30pm, though some stay open past midnight. Modern indoor restaurants generally have last kitchen orders by 10pm. Some hotel coffee shops stay open 24 hours, and the city has several outdoor restaurants that are open as late as 4am for after-hours suppers. Clubs and bars are subject to loosely applied licensing laws and may close anywhere between midnight and 5am, depending on location and political and policing climate.

C

Children

Thais love children, and will go out of their way to help in most situations should you need it. This might even stretch to waiters playing with your kids while you enjoy a restaurant meal.

Buying nappies, baby food and other supplies is straightforward, with department stores and chemists well stocked. Nappy-changing spaces are scarce, however, in Bangkok, some central department stores have facilities, and they may also have breastfeeding rooms.

Lugging a baby carrier around will feel like twice the weight in the tropical heat, so a light buggy may be a better option. That said, the pavements are very difficult to negotiate, often being cracked, full of holes and cluttered with street stalls and people, so some travellers prefer the option of a carrier. Only a handful of Skytrain stations have lifts, but all the metro stations do.

If you are hiring a car, international firms such as Budget (www.budget.co.th) have baby seats suitable for ages six months to three years in all locations, but you need to pre-book. There is a small extra charge. There are no car seats for younger children. Cars are fitted with mounting points if you take your own baby seats.

The tropical heat is intense, so sunblock and sunhats are important, while keeping hands clean helps to ward off stomach bugs.

Eating out

Dining with children in Thailand should be hassle free. Thais themselves don't feed their kids spicy food, and there are lots of dishes that are very mild. There is also a wide choice of international food available in the main tourist centres, including Western fast-food outlets. Most Thai places welcome children. For international restaurants it is worth calling ahead to check.

Accommodation

There is a growing range of facilities for children in medium-range hotels and upwards in Bangkok. Some hotels have a kids' pool and babysitting facilities, and resort-style hotels, in particular,

Khao San Road, a backpacker hub

may have child-dedicated clubs to take the strain while you go out and have some fun.

Climate

There are three seasons in Bangkok: hot (Mar–mid-June): 27–35°C (80–95°F); rainy (June–Oct): 24–32°C (75–90°F); cool (Nov–Feb): 18–32°C (65–90°F), and with less humidity.

Clothing

Clothes should be light, loose and preferably made of natural fibres, which breathe better. Shorts are fine to wear in most situations, although not in temples or palace grounds, where legs and shoulders should be covered. A shirt and tie are expected for business appointments. A hat will offer protection from the fierce sun, and it is obviously wise to carry an umbrella during the rainy season.

Crime and safety

Although Bangkok, like all cities, has an underbelly of violent crime, tourists rarely encounter it, and the streets are generally very safe. Thais tend to be non-confrontational, and the country is generally safe for women travellers in terms of both casual harassment and serious assault.

That said, it is best to avoid walking alone at night on beaches. The biggest risk to travellers is from scams and con artists. Beach destinations, including Pattaya, now have a major problem with claims that tourists have damaged jet skis, or other equipment. These disputes sometimes escalate into violence, and, with rampant corruption and bribery, the police response is usually unsatisfactory at best.

Following travel warnings by several western embassies, in 2013 the government set up dedicated tourist courts at Suvarnabhum airport and in Pattaya and Phuket, with possibly more to come. If you do run into trouble, contact the Tourist Police: Tourist Service Centre, TAT headquarters, 4 Thanon Ratchadamnoen Nok; tel: 0 2281 5051; hotline: 1155; http://tourist-police.go.th. Tourist police booths can be found in tourist areas, including Lumphini Park (near the intersection of Rama IV and Silom) and Patpong (at the Surawong intersection). Most tourist police speak some English.

Customs

The Thai government prohibits the import or export of drugs, dangerous chemicals, pornography, firearms, ammunition and goods that display the Thai flag. The maximum penalty for smuggling hard drugs is death.

Tourists have a duty-free allowance of 200 cigarettes and 1 litre of wine or spirits. Foreign currency over US$20,000 entering or leaving the country should be declared. Thai currency leaving the country is limited to B50,000.

VAT refunds are available on completion of necessary paperwork at the

Night market stall   *Traditional dance performers*

airport. Buddha images, antiques and art objects must have a Department of Fine Arts permit, which can be arranged by the vendor (or tel: 0 2224 1333). Pre-18th-century items must not be exported. Check www.customs.go.th, or call the hotline: 1164.

E

Electricity

Electrical outlets are rated at 220 volts, 50 cycles and accept flat- or round-pronged plugs. Adaptors are cheap to buy at department or hardware stores.

Embassies

Australia: 181 Wireless Road, Lumphini, tel: 0-2344 6300, https://thailand.embassy.gov.au.

Canada: 15/F, Abdulrahim Place, 990 Th. Rama IV, tel: 0-2646 4300, www.canadainternational.gc.ca/Thailand-thailande.

New Zealand: M Thai Tower, 14th Floor, All Seasons Place, 87 Wireless Road, tel: 0-2254 2530, www.mfat.govt.nz/en/countries-and-regions/south-east-asia/thailand/new-zealand-embassy.

Singapore: 129 Th. Sathorn Tai, tel: 0-2384 6700, www.mfa.gov.sg/bangkok.

UK: 14 Wireless Road, Lumphini, tel: 0-2305 8333, www.gov.uk/world/organisations/british-embassy-bangkok.

US: 95 Wireless Road, tel: 0-2205 4000, https://th.usembassy.gov.

Emergencies

Medical emergency: 1669.
Police: 191.
Direct ambulance number: 1669.
Direct fire number: 199.
Tourist Police: emergency hotline tel: 1155; or 0 2281 5051, or 0 2664 0222.

Etiquette

Thais are remarkably tolerant, but there are a few things that upset them:

Buddhism: It is impolite to point your feet at Buddha images or to have bare legs or shoulders when visiting temples. Monks have taken vows of celibacy, and women should avoid physical contact with them, including passing items directly to them. Instead, place the object somewhere to be picked up.

Head and feet: Thais believe the head and feet to be the highest and lowest parts of the body, spiritually as well as physically. It is therefore seen as insulting to touch another person's head, to move items with your feet, or to step over another person.

Intimacy: Public shows of affection rarely extend beyond holding hands.

Terms of address: Thais are addressed by their first names, usually preceded by the word *Khun*, the equivalent of Mr or Ms. For example, Silpachai Krishnamra would be addressed as Khun Silpachai.

Thai greetings: The common greeting and farewell in Thailand is *Sawasdee* (followed by *khrap* when spoken

STA	Airlines	Flight no.	From	ETA	Reclaim
19:25		FD 3725	HO CHI MINH	20:56	7
19:45		QZ 7716	JAKARTA	22:53	20
20:20		BG 0085	SINGAPORE	01:30	17
20:30		DD 0331	YANGON	23:00	15
20:30		NX 0882	MACAU	21:42	12

STA	Airlines	Flight no.	From	ETA	Reclaim
21:55		NH 5951	ไทเป	21:37	17
22:00		FD 3506	สิงคโปร์	21:56	16
22:00		SQ 0632	สิงคโปร์	21:36	16
22:00		RJ 9410	สิงคโปร์	22:42	12
22:05		KL 0878	โทเกียว	00:05	22

Suvarnabhumi Airport handles all international flights

by men and *kha* by women). In more formal settings this is accompanied by a *wai* – raising the hands in a prayer-like gesture, the fingertips touching the nose, and bowing the head slightly. In business meetings the *wai* is often followed by a handshake. Foreigners are not expected to *wai*.

The Royal Family: Thais have a great reverence for the monarchy, and disapprove of any disrespect directed towards members of the royal family. Thailand also has lèse-majesté laws that, although usually invoked to settle business or political rivalries, may result in jail terms for people convicted of defaming, insulting or threatening royalty. Standing for the national anthem is expected in cinemas regardless of your nationality.

H

Health

Visitors entering Thailand are not required to show evidence of vaccinations, but do check that tetanus boosters are up-to-date. Inoculations for cholera and hepatitis A and B are a good idea. When in border areas with Cambodia, Laos and Myanmar apply mosquito repellent on exposed skin at all times; ideally, cover up to protect against malaria and dengue fever.

It is important to drink plenty of water and use sunblock. Tap water in Bangkok has been certified drinkable, but bottled water is still safer and is easily available. Within Bangkok ice is clean and presents no health problems.

Hospitals and dental clinics: The standard of doctors, equipment and medical care at the following hospitals is excellent. All have English-speaking staff and additional specialised clinics, including dental facilities.

Bangkok Hospital: 2 Soonvijai Soi 7, New Petchburi; tel: 0 2310 3000; www.bangkokhospital.com.

BNH Hospital: 9/1 Thanon Convent, Silom; tel: 0 2686 2700; www.bnhhospital.com.

Bumrungrad Hospital: 33 Sukhumvit Soi 3, tel: 0 2667 1000; www.bumrungrad.com.

Medical clinics: For minor problems, MedConsult Clinic (The Racquet Club, Sukhumvit Soi 49/9; tel: 0 2762 7855; www.medconsultclinic.wordpress.com) is run by a native English-speaking general practitioner who will make house calls. Major hotels have an on-site clinic or a doctor on call.

Pharmacies: There are many branches of Boots and Watson's pharmacies in central Bangkok, including in shopping malls. Many antibiotics and other drugs are available without a prescription. Always check the expiry date.

I

Internet

Wi-Fi zones are a fast-growing and the government has announced commitments to increase them around the city.

Thai coins

They are currently found at the airport, in some hotels and at some coffee shops, including branches of Starbucks. Major hotel internet services usually include in-room; even smaller hotels sometimes have internet access available. Public internet cafés mainly have reasonable speed broadband for around B30 per hour. There are many located around Khao San Road. Otherwise, your hotel concierge should know the nearest available.

L

Language

English is widely used in hotels and shops, but it is always appreciated when visitors try to use some Thai. To be polite, men should end each sentence with the syllable *khrap*. Women should end each sentence with *kha*. Transliteration of Thai into the Roman alphabet is difficult, as there are only a few one-to-one phonological correspondences. For some more information on language and some general useful words and phrases, see page 134.

LGBTQ+ travellers

The LGBTQ+ nightlife scene is thriving and the city hosts an on-off Bangkok Gay Pride Festival in November. Details are often available about this and other events at www.travelgayasia.com. Find updates on the useful resource site www. utopia-asia.com or at Purple Dragon, a travel agency that caters exclusively for gay travellers (942/58 Charn Issara Tower 1, Thanon Rama IV; tel: 0 2236 1776; www.purpledrag.com).

Lost property

Report lost property as soon as possible to the Tourist Police (hotline: 1155) to get an insurance statement.

Suvarnabhumi Airport: tel: 0 2132 1888; **Don Mueang Airport:** tel: 0 2535 1253.

Public transit: BMTA city bus service, tel: 0 2246 0973; BTS Skytrain, tel: 0 2617 6000; MRTA subway, tel: 0 2624 6200, Hualamphong Railway Station, hotline: 1690.

Taxis: taxi hotline (tel: 1644); or JS100 Radio 100FM hotline (tel: 1137), to which taxi drivers often respond.

M

Maps

Basic maps of Bangkok are available free at the Tourism Authority of Thailand (TAT) offices (see page 128) and at big hotels. More detailed ones can be found in bookshops. The Insight Fleximap and *Nelles Map of Bangkok* are both good. The colourful hand-drawn *Nancy Chandler's Map of Bangkok* is good on local knowledge and has useful margin tips covering cultural attractions, markets, shops, etc.

Media

Newspapers and magazines: the *Bangkok Post* and *The Nation* are both English-language daily newspapers. The free

Bangkok postbox

weekly magazine, *BK* (https://bk.asia-city.com), keeps up with events around the city. The glossy small-format monthly *Bangkok 101* (www.bangkok101.com) costs B100, and has a good run down of art shows and venues, along with events and restaurant and nightlife reviews.

Radio: English-language stations come and go frequently. At the time of writing, options include Fat FM (104.5FM) and FMX (95.5FM).

Television: True Visions network has film, sport, news and entertainment channels such as HBO, ESPN, BBC World News and MTV Thailand.

Money

ATMs: These are available at banks, malls, major train and bus stations, and airports. Many accept credit cards and MasterCard and Visa debit cards.

Changing money: Banking hours are Mon–Fri 9.30am–3.30pm, but most banks maintain money-changing kiosks in tourist areas. Better hotels will change money, but generally at poor rates.

Credit cards: American Express, Diner's Club, MasterCard, JCB and Visa are widely accepted. Credit cards can be used to draw cash at most banks. If you lose your credit card, call:

American Express: tel: 0 2273 5222.
Diner's Club: tel: 0 2238 3660.
Visa: tel: 001 800 441 3485.
MasterCard: tel: 001 800 11-887 0663.

Credit card fraud is a major problem in Thailand. Do not leave your credit card in safe-deposit boxes. When mak-

ing a purchase, ensure you get the carbon copies and dispose of them. If you plan on using your credit card a lot, it may be worth taking an alternative one as a backup in case you run into problems through fraud or theft.

Local currency: The baht (B) is the principal Thai monetary unit, with banknote denominations of 1,000, 500, 100, 50 and 20. There are 10, 5, 2 and 1 baht, plus 50- (half baht/50 satang) and 25-satang coins.

Taxes: Thailand has a Value Added Tax (VAT) of 7 percent. This is added to most goods and services (but not goods sold by street vendors and markets). You can get the VAT refunded (see page 122), if your total purchases come to B5,000-worth of goods or more.

Major hotels add VAT and 10 percent service charge to the room rate, as do mid- to high-priced restaurants.

Tipping: Tipping is not a custom in Thailand, although it is common in upper-end establishments. However, people generally leave any loose change left over from their bill, both in food shops and taxis.

Traveller's cheques: These are gradually becoming less common and harder to change. They can be cashed at most exchange kiosks and banks, at a charge of B25 each.

P

Photography

Camera shops and photo-development outlets are commonly found in the tour-

Flowers at Erawan Shrine　　　*Check your mobile's service provider fees before using your phone abroad*

ist areas, and most offer digital transfers onto CD and hard copy photos from digital. Prints are available at B3–4 each, with bigger enlargements a real bargain.

Postal services

The Thai postal service is pretty reliable, though registering or sending items by EMS can improve the odds for domestic mail. Courier services are preferable for valuable parcels or bulky documents sent overseas.

The Central Post Office is located between Charoen Krung *sois* 32 and 34 (tel: 0 2233 1050; Mon–Fri 8am–8pm, Sat until 4pm and Sun and public holidays until 1pm). Post offices elsewhere in Bangkok usually open Mon–Fri 8am–4pm. The GPO and many larger offices sell packing boxes and materials.

Courier services:
DHL: tel: 0 2631 2621; www.dhl.co.th.
Fedex: tel: 0 2229 8800, or hotline: 1782; www.fedex.com/th.
UPS: tel: 0 2762 3300; www.ups.com/th.

Public holidays and festivals

1 Jan: New Year's Day
Late Feb/Mar: (full moon) Magha Puja. Note: Chinese New Year is not an official holiday, but many businesses close for several days
6 Apr: Chakri Day (or following Monday if the 6th falls on a weekend)
13–15 Apr: Songkran

1 May: Labour Day
Early May: Royal Ploughing Ceremony (officials only)
Late May/June: (full moon) Visakha Puja
28 July: H.M. King's birthday
Late July/Aug: (full moon) Asanha Puja and Khao Pansa
12 Aug: Queen's Birthday (Mothers' Day)
14 Oct: The passing of King Bhumibol
23 Oct: King Chulalongkorn Day
5 Dec: King's Birthday (Fathers' Day)
10 Dec: Constitution Day

Many festivals vary according to lunar cycles; for exact dates check with the Tourism Authority of Thailand (tel: 0 2250 5500; www.tourismthailand.org). Some of the bigger festivals are: late Feb/Mar full moon: Magha Puja; Mar/Apr: kite-flying season; early Oct: Vegetarian Festival; Nov full moon: Loy Krathong.

R

Religion

Although it is predominantly Buddhist, Thailand has historically been tolerant of other religions. Buddhist temples are plentiful and there are several mosques, a major Hindu temple and a handful of Christian churches and synagogues.

Anglican and Episcopalian: Christ Church Bangkok, 11 Convent Road; tel: 0 2234 3634; www.christchurchbangkok.org. Sunday services at 7.30am, 10am and 5pm.

Hualamphong railway station

Catholic: Holy Redeemer Church, 123/19 Soi Ruam Rudi, Thanon Withayu; tel: 0 2651 5251; www.holyredeemerbangkok.net. Sunday mass at 8.30am, 9.45am, 11am and 5.30pm.

Jewish: Even Chen Synagogue, Chao Phraya Office Tower, Shangri-La Hotel, Charoen Krung Soi 42/1; tel: 08 1917 3754. Services daily at 9am.

Muslim: Assalafiyah Mosque, 2827 Thanon Charoen Krung; tel: 0 2688 1481. Service times vary.

T

Telephones

International calls: The country code for Thailand is 66. When calling Thailand from overseas, dial your local international access code, followed by 66 and the 8-digit number (without the preceding 0). To make an international call from Thailand, dial 001 or 009 before the country and area codes, followed by the telephone number. For international call assistance, dial 100.

Prepaid phone cards (Thaicard) for international calls are available at post offices and shops with the Thaicard sign.

Local calls: Area codes in Thailand are merged with phone numbers. The prefix 0 must be dialled for all calls made within Thailand, even when calling local numbers in Bangkok. Dial 0 first, followed by the 8-digit number. For local directory assistance, dial 1133.

Any number that begins with 08 is a local mobile number.

Public telephones: These accept B1, B5 and B10 coins. Phonecards for local calls (B50, B100, B200 and B400) are available at convenience shops: there are several available, some are cheaper, particularly for international calls. Call the phone company hotlines for options (CAT, tel: 1322; TOT, tel: 1100).

Time difference

Thailand is 7 hours ahead of GMT. Since it gets dark between 6–7pm uniformly throughout the year, Thailand does not observe daylight saving time.

Tourist information

The Tourism Authority of Thailand (TAT) has offices in several countries and kiosks within Thailand that offer maps and other promotional materials, as well as advice on things to do and places to see. The website www.tourismthailand.org has plenty of information, although much of it is outdated and not necessarily kept current.

TAT Call Centre: tel: 1672; daily 8am–8pm.

TAT Main Office: 1600 Thanon New Phetchaburi, Makkasan, Bangkok 10400; tel: 0 2250 5500; daily 8.30am–4.30pm.

TAT Tourist Information Counters: Arrivals Hall, Suvarnabhumi Airport; tel: 0 2504 2701; daily 8am–10pm; 4 Thanon Ratchadamnoen Nok; tel: 0 2282 9774; daily 8.30am–4.30pm.

Traffic jam *Tuk tuks awaiting passengers*

Overseas offices
Australia and New Zealand: Suite 2002, Level 20, 56 Pitt Street, Sydney, NSW 2000; tel: +61 2 9247 7549.
UK: 1st Floor, 17–19 Cockspur Street, Trafalgar Square, London SW1Y 5BL; tel: +44 20 7925 2511.
US: 61 Broadway, Suite 2810, New York, NY 10006; tel: +1 212 432 0433; and 611 North Larchmont Boulevard, 1st Floor, Los Angeles, CA 90004; tel: +1 323 461 9814.

Transport

Getting there
By air: Bangkok's Suvarnabhumi Airport (tel: 0 2132 1888; www.suvarnabhumiairport.com) is located about 30km (19 miles) east of Bangkok. The airport handles most international flights to Bangkok as well as many domestic connections.

Some low-budget carriers use Bangkok's old Don Mueang Airport (tel: 0 2535 1111; www.donmuangairportonline.com) for both domestic and international flights, including Air Asia (www.airasia.com/th/en), Orient Thai (www.flyorientthai.com) and Nok Air (www.nokair.com). Don Mueang is about 30km (19 miles) north of the city centre.

It takes around 45 minutes, depending on traffic, to get to or from either airport to the city by taxi. The Suvarnabhumi Airport Rail Link connects that airport with the city and there are also BMTA public buses from both airports, plus train connections from Don Mueang; check the website for details.

There are two left luggage facilities at Suvarnabhumi Airport on the second and fourth floors. The fee is B100 per piece per day. Hotels and guest houses offer a left-luggage service, usually for a small daily fee.

By rail: The State Railway of Thailand (tel: hotline: 1690; www.railway.co.th) operates trains that are generally clean, cheap and reliable. There are three entry points by rail into Thailand. Two are from Malaysia, the more popular of which is the daily train that leaves Butterworth near Penang at 1.15pm for Hat Yai (south Thailand) and arrives in Bangkok's Hualamphong Station at 10.50am the next morning. Trains leave Hualamphong daily at 2.45pm for Malaysia. There is also a short line from Nong Khai, in northeast Thailand, to 3km (2 miles) across the Laos border. This will eventually extend to Vientiane.

By road: Malaysia provides the main road access into Thailand, with crossings near Betong and Sungai Kolok. From Laos, there four Friendship Bridges, at Mukdahan, Nakhon Phanom and Nong Khai, all in northeast Thailand, and at Chiang Khong, in Chiang Rai Province. There is also a land crossing at Huay Kon (in Nan Province). From Cambodia the most commonly used border crossing is from Poipet. Another option is to go overland from Kompong Cham in Cambodia, crossing over to Hat Lek in Thailand.

Longtail boats

Getting around

Metro: Bangkok's underground MRT stations stretch between Bang Sue, in the northern suburbs, and the city's main railway station, Hualamphong, at the edge of Chinatown. Three stations – Silom, Sukhumvit and Chatuchak Park – link to the BTS network. The air-conditioned trains operate from 6am to midnight (every 2–4 minutes peak, 4–6 minutes off-peak). Fares start at B16, increasing B2–3 every station, with a maximum fare of B41.

Buy coin-sized plastic tokens at kiosks or self-service ticket machines. Passes are also available for unlimited journeys: 1-day (B120), 3-day (B230), 30-day (B1,400), plus a stored-value adult card (B230, which includes a B80 deposit and issuing fee).

Customer relations centre: tel: 0 2624 5200; www.mrta.co.th/en.

Skytrain: The Bangkok Transit System (BTS) elevated train service, also known as the Skytrain, is the perfect way to beat the traffic. It has two routes: Sukhumvit Line and Silom Line, which intersect at Siam Station. Trains operate from 6am to midnight (every 3 minutes peak, 5 minutes off-peak). Single-trip fares are B15–42 according to distance. It is useful to buy the 1-day pass (B130; unlimited journeys), and there's a Rabbit Card to which you can add discounted multi-trip packages running from B405 for 15 trips to B1,100 for 50 trips. The Rabbit Card is valid on the BRT and may eventually extend to the MRT. BTS Tourist Information Centres (tel: 0 2617 7341; hotline: 0 2617 6000; www.bts.co.th) are found on the concourse levels of Siam, Phaya Thai and Saphan Taksin stations (daily 8am–8pm).

Taxi: Metered air-conditioned taxis are inexpensive, and comfortably seat 3–4 people. It is best to hail them on the streets; those parked outside hotels usually hustle for a no-meter fare.

The fare is B35 for the first kilometre, then B5–8.50 per kilometre, depending on distance travelled. If stuck in traffic, a small per-minute surcharge kicks in. If your journey crosses town, ask the driver to take the expressway. The toll fare of B25–45 is given to the driver at the payment booth, not at the end of the trip.

Before starting, check that the meter has been reset and turned on. Fares can be negotiated for longer distances outside Bangkok: for instance, to Pattaya (B1,200), Koh Samet (B1,500) or Hua Hin (B1,500–2,000). Drivers often don't speak much English, but should know the locations of major hotels. It is a good idea to have a destination written in Thai.

Siam Taxi (hotline: 1661) will take bookings for a B20 surcharge.

Motorcycle taxi: Stands for motorcycle taxis are noticeable by their drivers – a gathering of men in fluorescent numbered vests found at the mouth of many *sois*, at busy intersections, buildings and markets. Hire only a driver

The Skytrain   *Cruising through Bangkok*

who provides a passenger helmet, and negotiate fares beforehand. Motorcycle taxis are a great way to beat the traffic and economical for short journeys like the length of a street, which will cost B10–20. A B80–100 ride should get you a half-hour trip across most parts of the downtown area. During rush hour (7–9am and 4–6pm), prices are higher. If the driver is going too fast, ask him to slow down: *cha-cha khap/kha*.

Tuk tuk: Few drivers of these brightly coloured three-wheeled taxis speak English, so best to have your destination written in Thai. Negotiate the fare before you set off. Expect to pay B30–50 for short journeys of a few blocks or 15 minutes, and B50–100 for longer journeys. B100 should get you a half-hour trip across most parts of the downtown area. Although they can be a fun experience, tuk tuk fares are rarely lower than metered taxis, and you ride in the midst of all the traffic fumes.

Bus: Buses are very cheap, but with little English spoken by staff or displayed on signage, finding the right bus can be frustrating. Municipal and private operators all come under the charge of the Bangkok Mass Transit Authority (BMTA; tel: 0 2246 0973; www.bmta.co.th). Free maps found at the airport and tourist centres often have bus routes marked.

The Bus Rapid Transit (BRT) system uses dedicated lanes, but at present is limited to a single route from Chong Nonsi BTS station to Wong Wian Yai on the Thonburi side of the river.

Boat: The Chao Phraya Express Boat Company (tel: 0 2623 6143; www.chaophrayaexpressboat.com/en) runs several services between Nonthaburi Pier in the north to Ratburana in the south. Boats run every 15 minutes from 6am to 7pm, and stop at different piers according to the coloured flag on top of the boat. Yellow and green flags are fastest, but stop at only 12 piers, while orange flags are slowest but stop at every pier. On Saturday and Sunday there are only orange-flag services. Tickets cost B10–40 and are purchased from the conductor on board or at some pier counters.

The company also runs charters and the Chao Phraya Tourist Boat, which operates daily from 9.30am to 4pm, for B150 a ticket for unlimited rides (which you can also use after 4pm on regular express boats). A useful commentary is provided on board, along with a small guidebook and a bottle of water. The route begins at the Tha Sathorn (Sathom Pier) and travels upriver to the Tha Phra Athit, with 10 stops in between. Boats leave every 30 minutes.

There are also cross-river ferries close to the piers that service the Chao Phraya River Express Boats. Costing B3.5 per journey, they operate from 5am to 10pm, or later.

Longtail boat taxis ply the river and narrow inner canals, carrying passengers from the centre of town to the outskirts. Many piers are located near road

Jams at the Chong Nonsi intersection

bridges. Tell the conductor your destination, as boats do not stop otherwise. Tickets cost B5–10, depending on distance, with services operating roughly every 10 minutes until 6–7pm. Visitors will probably only need the main downtown canal, Khlong Saen Saep, which travels from Tha Saphan Phanfah, near Wat Saket, into the heart of the downtown area and on to Bang Kapi. It can be a useful route to Jim Thompson's House, Siam Centre and the Thanon Ploenchit malls.

If you wish to explore the canals of Thonburi or Nonthaburi, private long-tail boats can be hired from most of the river's main piers. A 90-minute to two-hour tour will take you into the quieter canal communities. Enquire beforehand which route the boat will take and what will be seen along the way, and negotiate rates (B700–800 for an hour, B1,000 and over for two hours). The price is for the entire boat, which may seat up to 16 people. On the trip, ask to pull up and get out if anything interests you.

Car rental: Thailand has a good road system, with signs in both Thai and English, and driving is largely comfortable, although with a few caveats. Tailgating and hazardous overtaking are common, lane discipline is erratic, and right of way is often determined by size. Motorcycles are numerous, so the use of mirrors needs to be constant.

An international driver's licence is required if you drive in Thailand. Car rental starts around B800 a day (check that insurance is included), but it is worth phoning around, as prices vary greatly.
Avis: 2/12 Thanon Withayu; tel: 0 2255 5300-4; and Suvarnabhami Airport (arrival hall 2); tel: 0 84 700 8157–9; Reservation Centre, tel: 0 2251 1131–2; www.avisthailand.com.
Hertz: Sukhumvit Soi 71; tel: 0 2266 4666; www.hertz.com.
Sathorn Car Rent: 6/8–9 Thanon Sathorn; tel: 0 2633 8888.

If you are not confident, car or van rental with a driver is available for an extra B300–500 per day, plus a surcharge if an overnight stay is included. For these try Thai Car Hire (www.thaicarhire.com) or Krungthai Car Rent (tel: 0 2291 8888; www.krungthai.co.th).

Travellers with disabilities

Bangkok falls short on accommodating people with disabilities. The uneven pavements are studded with obstructions, and few buildings have wheelchair ramps. Traffic is relentless, and drivers are generally unsympathetic to pedestrians. However, there have been signs of improvement in recent years. Only a few Skytrain stations have lifts, but the metro has them at every station, and more expensive hotels and shopping malls often have disabled access and modified toilets. Taxi drivers, if arranged beforehand, can be quite cooperative. However, it may be preferable to travel with a companion. Online resources are somewhat thin on the

Currency exchange office

ground. There are some companies that can help with things such as accessible hotels and local carers or assistants, as well as planning tours, such as Wheelchair Holidays Thailand: www.wheelchairtours.com.

V

Visas and passports

Travellers should check visa regulations at a Thai embassy or consulate before starting their trip, as visa rules vary for different nationalities. For an updated list, check the Thai Ministry of Foreign Affairs website at www.mfa.go.th/main/en.

All foreign nationals entering Thailand must have valid passports with at least six months before the expiry date. Nationals from most countries are granted either visa exemption or visas on arrival at the airport, valid for 15–90 days, depending on the country. Officially, you need an air ticket out of Thailand, but this is rarely checked. Longer tourist visas, obtained from the Thai consulate in your home country prior to arrival, allow a 60-day stay.

Visas can be extended for 30 days at a time for B1,000 at the Immigration Bureau (120 Moo 3, Thanon Chaengwattana; tel: 0 2141 9889; www.immigration.go.th; Mon–Fri 8.30am–4.30pm), or you can leave the country (even for half an hour) and return in order to receive another visa on entry. In total, tourists are allowed to stay in Thailand for a cumulative period

not exceeding 90 days within any six-month period from the date of first entry.

People seeking a work permit can apply for a non-immigrant visa, which is good for 90 days. A letter of guarantee is needed from the Thai company you intend to work for, and this visa can be obtained from a Thai consulate at home.

Overstaying your visa carries a daily fine of B500 up to a maximum of B20,000, which is payable at the airport on leaving. However, staying in Thailand on an expired visa is against the law, and if the police catch you before you leave you may be jailed and deported.

W

Websites

Bangkok Post: www.bangkokpost.com. The country's biggest-selling, English-language daily newspaper.

BK Magazine: www.bkmagazine.com. Site of a weekly listings magazine with features, events and restaurant reviews.

Khaosan Road: www.khaosanroad.com. Backpacker resource with accommodation, forums, etc.

Langhub: www.langhub.com/en-th. Audio and video files to learn Thai.

Siam2Nite: www.siam2nite.com. All the latest nightlife events.

TAT: www.tourismthailand.org. Official tourist authority website.

Time Out: www.timeout.com/bangkok/restaurants. Reviews of restaurants and bars in Bangkok.

Train sign reading 'Chiang Mai–Bangkok'

LANGUAGE

Thai language's roots go back to the place Thais originated – the hills of southern China – but it is also overlaid by Indian influences. From the original settlers come the five tones (see below) that seem to frustrate new learners. These tones each change the meaning of a sound, so when you mispronounce a word, you say another word entirely. It is not unusual to see a semi-fluent foreigner standing before a Thai and running through the scale of tones until suddenly a light of recognition dawns on the latter's face. Despite the confusions, any attempt at communicating in Thai is usually gratefully received. Note there is no universal transliteration system from Thai into English. Place and road names may be written slightly differently from how they appear in this book. To be polite, questions should be followed by 'khap' if you're male and 'kha' if you're female.

The five tones

Mid tone (no symbol): voiced at the speaker's normal, even pitch.
High tone (h): pitched slightly higher than the mid tone.
Low tone (l): pitched slightly lower than the mid tone.
Rising tone (r): sounds like a questioning pitch, starting low and rising.
Falling tone (f): sounds like an English speaker suddenly understanding something: 'Oh, I see!'

General

Hello, goodbye Sa (l) wa (l) dee (a man then says khrap; a woman says kha, thus sawadee khrap or sawadee kha)
How are you? Khun sa (l) bai dii, mai (h)
Well, thank you Sa (l) bai dii, khopkhun
Thank you very much Khop (l) khun maak (h)
I cannot speak Thai Phuut Thai mai (f) dai (f)
I can speak a little Phuut Thai dai (f) nit (h) diew
yes chai (f)
no mai (f) chai (f)
Do you have…? Mii…mai (h)
How much? Thao (f) rai
expensive phaeng
Can you lower the price a bit? Kaw lot noi dai (f) mai (h)
Do you have another colour? Mii sii uhn mai (h)
I don't want it Mai ao
hot (heat hot) rawn (h)
hot (spicy) phet
cold yen
I do not feel well Mai (f) sabai

Numbers

0 soon
1 neung
2 song (r)
3 sam (r)
4 sii
5 haa (f)

6 *hok*
7 *jet*
8 *bet*
9 *kow (f)*
10 *sip*
11 *sip et*
12 *sip song (r)*
13 *sip sam (r) and so on*
20 *yii sip*
30 *sam sip (f, m) and so on*
100 *neung roi*
1,000 *neung phan*

Getting around

where *thii (f) nai (r)*
right *khwaa (r)*
left *sai (h)*
turn *leo*
straight ahead *trong pai*
please slow down *cha cha noi*
stop here *jawt thii (f) nii (f)*
fast *raew*
slow *cha*
hotel *rong raem*
street *thanon*
lane *soi*
bridge *saphan*
police station *sathanii dtam ruat*
ferry *reua*
longtail boat *reua haang yao*
train *rot fai*
bus *rot may*
Skytrain *rot fai faa*
metro/subway *rot fai tai din*

Online

Where's an internet cafe? *internet cafaire (r) yoo thii (f) nai (r)*

Does it have wireless internet? *mii wifi mai (h)*
What is the Wi-Fi password? *password wifi keur arai*
Is the Wi-Fi free? *wifi thii (f) nii (f) free mai (h)*
Can I access the internet? *mii internet mai (h)*
Can I access Skype? *mii Skype mai (h)*
Can I...? *...dai mai (h)*
check email *check email*
print *prin*
plug in/charge my laptop/iPhone/iPad? *kaw seap plag/charge laptop/iPhone/iPad*
How much per hour/half hour? *cheua mong neung/kreung cheua mong thao (f) rai*
How do I...? *...yang (f) nai*
connect/disconnect *connec/disconnec*
log on/log off *log on/log off*
What's your email? *email kong khun keur arai (f)*
My email is... *email kawng pom (male)/dichan (female) keur...*

Social media

Are you on Facebook/Twitter? *khun mii facebook/twitteure (r)*
What's your user name? *user name kawng khun (h) arai (f)*
I'll add you as a friend *ja add khun phen peuan (h)*
I'll follow you on Twitter *ja dtham khun nai twitteure (r)*
I'll put the pictures on Facebook/Twitter *ja post roob nai facebook/twitteure (r)*

Depiction of the Ramakien

BOOKS AND FILM

Much of the country's classical written literature was destroyed when the Burmese sacked Ayutthaya in 1767. The Thais have since then placed a heavy emphasis on the oral tradition. At the heart of Thai literature is the *Ramakien*, the Thai version of the Indian *Ramayana*, and the *Jataka* tales, also of Indian origin, which tell of the Buddha's reincarnations prior to enlightenment. The first tales were translated from Pali script to Thai in the late 15th century. They have generated many popular and classic stories, such as *Phra Aphaimani*, by Sunthorn Phu, the 18th-century equivalent of poet laureate.

Thai novels were first published in the 1920s, with mainly social or political themes. Military rule in the 1950s, however, brought heavy censorship, and quality fiction practically disappeared for 20 years. Many landmark Thai books were translated into English in the early 1990s. The late prime minister and cultural advocate Kukrit Pramoj's *Many Lives*, for instance, gives a good introduction to the Buddhist way of thinking. His *Four Reigns* is a fictional yet accurate account of court life in the 19th and 20th centuries. Also of note are Kampoon Boontawee's *Children of Isaan* and *Botan's Letters from Thailand*.

Like most places in the world, Hollywood blockbusters dominate the cinemas, and most independent Thai films don't get the screen time they deserve.

This is a shame, as there are some talented Thai directors receiving acclaim on the international circuit. Leading the way is Apichatpong Weerasethakul, who has won three Cannes prizes, including the Palme d'Or in 2010 for *Uncle Boonmee Who Can Recall His Past Lives*.

The city's annual film festivals include the Bangkok International Film Festival (https://bangiff2017.wixsite.com/bangiff1) and World Film Festival (www.worldfilmbkk.com).

Books

Art and culture
Thai Folk Wisdom: Contemporary Takes on Traditional Proverbs by Tulaya Pornpiriyakulchai and Jane Vejjajiva. Dual-language coffee table book that looks at society through 50 proverbs. Illustrated with paintings by leading Thai artists.
Things Thai by Tanistha Dansilp and Michael Freeman. Quintessential Thai objects and artefacts.
Very Thai: Everyday Popular Culture by Philip Cornwell-Smith. If you've ever wondered why every compound in Thailand has a spirit house, or why insect treats are such a hit, this book is for you.

Fiction
Bangkok Haunts by John Burdett. More hard-boiled capers with the half-Thai, half-American Buddhist policeman of

The 2010 Thai film 'Uncle Boonmee Who Can Recall His Past Lives'

Bangkok 8 fame.

The Beach by Alex Garland. The beach read that inspired the film starring Leonardo DiCaprio, about backpackers trying to find their own paradise.

Many Lives (Lai Chiwit) by Kukrit Pramoj. Insight into Buddhist thought from the famous Thai polymath.

Food

Thai Food by David Thompson. Almost 700 pages of traditional recipes with background on food and social fabric from the chef who launched the restaurant Nahm, in London and Bangkok.

General

Mai Pen Rai Means Never Mind by Carol Hollinger. Reprint of amusing personal experiences in Thailand half a century ago.

Travellers' Tales Thailand edited by James O'Reilly and Larry Habegger. A collection of stimulating observations and true stories from around 50 writers.

History and society

A History of Buddhism in Siam by Prince Dhani Nivat. Written by one of Thailand's most respected scholars.

A History of Thailand by Dr Pasuk Phongpaichit and Chris Baker. Concise history of the country, mainly from the Rattanakosin period.

A Journalist in Siam by Andrew A Freeman. Take a trip back in time with this 1920s travelogue by the then-editor of the *Bangkok Daily Mail* newspaper.

The King Never Smiles: A Biography of Thailand's Bhumibol Adulyadej by Paul M. Handley. An unauthorised portrait of the current King Bhumibol. As monarchy matters are taken very seriously, the book is banned in the kingdom and throughout Southeast Asia.

Film

The Bridge on the River Kwai (1957). A fictionalised account of Allied POWs building the bridge, which still stands in Kanchanaburi, as part of the World War II Japanese railway link with Burma.

Dang Birely's Young Gangsters (1997). A violent film set in 1956 based on real life turf wars between young gangs.

Tears of the Black Tiger (2001). The first Thai film to make the official selection at Cannes is a kitsch homage to Thai melodrama.

Suriyothai (2001). The most expensive film ever made in Thailand tells the story of an Ayutthaya-period queen who sacrificed her life to save the king.

Tropical Malady (2004). An experimental film portraying a gay man searching for his lover who has transformed into a tiger in the jungle.

Uncle Boonmee Who Can Recall His Past Lives (2010). Cannes Palme D'Or winner about death and reincarnation. An ailing man recalls his previous lives.

Only God Forgives (2013). Ultra-violent offering from the pairing of Nicolas Winding Refn and Ryan Gosling about the city's complex criminal underworld.

ABOUT THIS BOOK

This *Explore Guide* has been produced by the editors of Insight Guides, whose books have set the standard for visual travel guides since 1970. With top-quality photography and authoritative recommendations, these guidebooks bring you the very best routes and itineraries in the world's most exciting destinations.

BEST ROUTES

The routes in the book provide something to suit all budgets, tastes and trip lengths. As well as covering the destination's many classic attractions, the itineraries track lesser-known sights, and there are also excursions for those who want to extend their visit outside the city. The routes embrace a range of interests, so whether you are an art fan, a gourmet, a history buff or have kids to entertain, you will find an option to suit.

We recommend reading the whole of a route before setting out. This should help you to familiarise yourself with it and enable you to plan where to stop for refreshments – options are shown in the 'Food and Drink' box at the end of each tour.

For our pick of the tours by theme, consult Recommended Routes for… (see pages 6–7).

INTRODUCTION

The routes are set in context by this introductory section, giving an overview of the destination to set the scene, plus background information on food and drink, shopping and more, while a succinct history timeline highlights the key events over the centuries.

DIRECTORY

Also supporting the routes is a Directory chapter, with a clearly organised A–Z of practical information, our pick of where to stay while you are there and select restaurant listings; these eateries complement the more low-key cafés and restaurants that feature within the routes and are intended to offer a wider choice for evening dining. Also included here are some nightlife listings, plus a handy language guide and our recommendations for books and films about the destination.

ABOUT THE AUTHORS

The original author of this book is the late Howard Richardson, who lived beside Bangkok's Chao Phraya River, and worked as a magazine editor and freelance writer. This edition was thoroughly updated by Insight regular Paul Stafford, who has travelled extensively throughout Thailand.

CONTACT THE EDITORS

We hope you find this Explore Guide useful, interesting and a pleasure to read. If you have any questions or feedback on the text, pictures or maps, please do let us know. If you have noticed any errors or outdated facts, or have suggestions for places to include on the routes, we would be delighted to hear from you. Please drop us an email at hello@insightguides.com. Thanks!

CREDITS

Explore Bangkok
Editor: Sian Marsh
Author: Howard Richardson
Head of DTP and Pre-Press: Rebeka Davies
Layout: Aga Bylica
Updated By: Paul Stafford
Managing Editor: Carine Tracanelli
Picture Editor: Tom Smyth and Aude Vauconsant
Cartography: original cartography Berndston & Berndston and Phoenix Mapping, updated by Carte

Photo credits: Alamy 24, 108, 109, 112; Apa Publications 4MC, 4ML, 6ML, 7MR, 7MR, 8ML, 8MC, 8MR, 8MR, 12, 12/13, 16/17, 17L, 18, 20, 22, 22/23, 26ML, 26MR, 30/31, 34, 36, 37L, 38, 40, 40/41, 41L, 42/43, 43L, 44, 46, 47, 49, 52, 54, 56, 57, 58, 59, 60/61, 66/67, 67L, 68, 70, 71L, 72, 74, 75L, 74/75, 80/81, 86, 89L, 90, 91, 112/113, 116, 117L, 120, 120/121, 121L, 124, 126, 126/127, 133, 136; Corbis 102, 110, 111; Dreamstime 100; Fotolia 134; Getty Images 104, 113L, 114, 115, 118, 127L; Grand Hyatt Erawan 103; Hans Fonk 62; iStock 1, 4MR, 4MR, 4/5T, 6TL, 7M, 8ML, 8MC, 8/9T, 10, 13L, 14/15, 16, 20/21, 26MC, 26ML, 26MC, 26MR, 26/27T, 31L, 32/33, 34/35, 35L, 38/39, 39L, 42, 45, 48, 50, 53, 60, 63, 68/69, 69L, 70/71, 76, 77, 83, 84/85, 85L, 88, 88/89, 92/93, 93L, 94, 94/95, 95L, 96, 97, 98MR, 98MR, 98ML, 98/99T, 101, 122, 123L, 125, 128, 128/129, 130, 131L, 135; Kobal 137; Mandarin Oriental Bangkok 106; Peter Stuckings/Apa Publications 4ML, 4MC, 6BC, 7T, 14, 15L, 19, 21L, 23L, 28, 29, 30, 36/37, 54/55, 55L, 61L, 64, 64/65, 66, 78, 79, 82, 86/87, 87L, 92, 98ML, 98MC, 116/117, 119, 122/123, 129L, 130/131, 132; Sheraton Grande Sukhumvit 105; Shutterstock 6MC, 11, 25, 51, 65L, 73, 84, 98MC; The Sukkothai 107
Cover credits: AWL Images (main) iStock (bottom)

Printed by RR Donnelley – China

DISTRIBUTION

UK, Ireland and Europe
Apa Publications (UK) Ltd
sales@insightguides.com
United States and Canada
Ingram Publisher Services
ips@ingramcontent.com
Australia and New Zealand
Woodslane
info@woodslane.com.au
Southeast Asia
Apa Publications (Singapore) Pte
singaporeoffice@insightguides.com
Worldwide
Apa Publications (UK) Ltd
sales@insightguides.com

SPECIAL SALES, CONTENT LICENSING AND COPUBLISHING

Insight Guides can be purchased in bulk quantities at discounted prices. We can create special editions, personalised jackets and corporate imprints tailored to your needs.
sales@insightguides.com
www.insightguides.biz

INDEX